101 MANDOLIN TIPS

STUFF ALL THE PROS KNOW AND USE

BY FRED SOKOLOW

with editorial assistance by Ronny Schiff

To access audio visit:
www.halleonard.com/mylibrary

Enter Code
3930-7174-2945-0611

Recording Credits
Fred Sokolow: Mandolin, other instruments, and vocals
Recorded and mixed at Sossity Sound by Michael Monagan
Some photos courtesy of Gold Tone.

ISBN 978-1-4803-4322-1

HAL•LEONARD®
CORPORATION
7777 W. BLUEMOUND RD. P.O. BOX 13819 MILWAUKEE, WI 53213

In Australia Contact:
Hal Leonard Australia Pty. Ltd.
4 Lentara Court
Cheltenham, Victoria, 3192 Australia
Email: ausadmin@halleonard.com.au

Visit Hal Leonard Online at
www.halleonard.com

INTRODUCTION

The mandolin evolved from the lute family in Italy and has been around for centuries. In recent years, it has become more visible due to its use in pop, country, progressive bluegrass, and American and English roots music bands such as Mumford and Sons, Arcade Fire, Taylor Swift, Yonder Mountain String Band, The Waybacks, and Death Cab for Cutie. However, using the mandolin in popular music is nothing new. It was also featured prominently in the 1960s,1970s, and 1980s by rock artists Led Zeppelin, Rod Stewart, the Grateful Dead, REM, and others.

In fact, the mandolin has contributed to practically all musical genres over the years, from the Baroque period, 18th and 19th century Italian popular music and opera, to early 20th century blues, ragtime, and rural string band music in the U.S. Mandolin was pivotal in the inception of bluegrass in the late 1940s and has been a mainstay in country music too. It is also important in Brazilian *choro* music—currently experiencing a world revival—and has a place in the musical traditions of Japan, India, Greece, and Venezuela.

What it comes down to is this: You can play any kind of music on the mandolin that you can think of. This little eight-stringed instrument has had quite an impact and its story is documented right here. In this volume you'll learn about: the history of the mandolin, which players have made it come alive, care and maintenance of the instrument, essential accessories, playing and practicing tips, and where to find mandolin groups, camps, festivals, and websites. It's a thorough introduction to the whole world of mandolin.

If you love the sound of the mandolin, read on. Hopefully, you'll use this book (and the accompanying audio tracks) to become a well-rounded and informed mandolin player!

Good luck,

Fred Sokolow

Fred Sokolow

ABOUT THE AUTHOR

Fred Sokolow is best known as the author of over 150 instructional and transcription books and DVDs for guitar, banjo, dobro, mandolin, and ukulele. Fred has long been a well-known West Coast multi-string performer and recording artist, particularly on the acoustic music scene. The diverse musical genres covered in his books and DVDs, along with several bluegrass, jazz, and rock albums he has released, demonstrate his mastery of many musical styles. Whether he's playing Delta bottleneck blues, bluegrass or old-time mandolin, '30s swing guitar or screaming rock solos, he does it with authenticity and passion.

Besides playing mandolin in bluegrass and country bands, he has wielded the instrument in such unusual settings as the *Tonight Show* Band, Disney television shows and videos, and a Rick James recording session. Fred is also the author of *Fretboard Roadmaps – Mandolin* (Book/CD, Hal Leonard).

Email Fred with any questions about this or his other books at: Sokolowmusic.com.

TABLE OF CONTENTS

Tip		Page

1 PARTS OF THE MANDOLIN

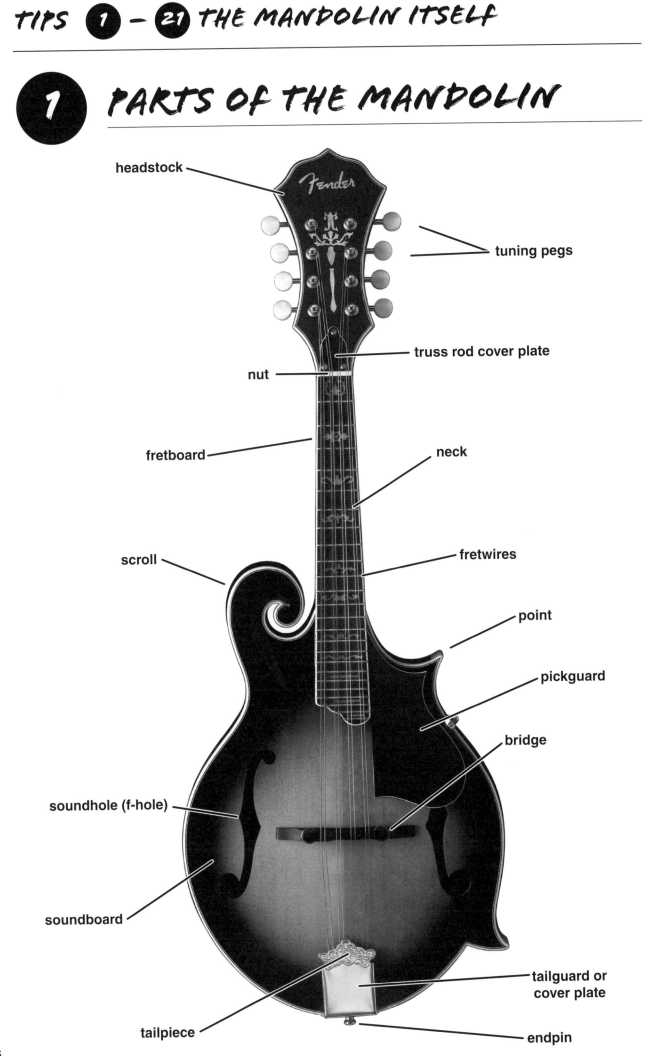

headstock

tuning pegs

truss rod cover plate

nut

fretboard

neck

scroll

fretwires

point

pickguard

bridge

soundhole (f-hole)

soundboard

tailguard or cover plate

tailpiece

endpin

2 ROUNDBACK MANDOLINS

Also called bowl-backed, the Neapolitan (roundback) mandolin has a bowl-shaped body made from strips of wood. The flat top is often bent back at the bridge to help the body support metal string tension (see the photo above). The fretboard joins the body at the 10th fret and there are usually seventeen frets in all. Elaborate, tortoise shell pickguards are often decorated with an inlaid pearl design. This basic design comes from the Vinaccia family of Naples, around the mid-1700s, and was further refined in the late 1800s by the Calace family.

The Neapolitan mandolin pre-dates the American, flat-bodied mandolin by nearly two centuries. In the early 1900s, Gibson, who pioneered the flat-bodied mandolin, nicknamed bowl-backed mandolins "tater bugs" because the striped effect of the different color wood strips resembles the back of the Colorado beetle or the rear segment of the potato bug.

3 A MODEL MANDOLINS

The flat-bodied A model mandolin, developed by Gibson at the beginning of the 20th century, has all but replaced the roundback style in the U.S. Gibson's teardrop shaped, flat-bodied, A models have an oval soundhole and a carved top and back. Some later models have f-holes, like a violin. Though Gibson's teardrop shape has been widely imitated, some companies have manufactured flat-bodied mandolins without a carved top or back.

The earliest A models had "The Gibson" printed on the headstock, but by the late 1920s, it was reduced to just "Gibson." They were available in natural wood, or painted black or white and are said to have a mellower, softer sound than the F models (see Tip #4).

F MODEL MANDOLINS

F stands for *Florentine*. Like the A models, the F model mandolins were designed by Orville Gibson around 1900. F model mandolins feature a scroll on the body and the headstock and usually two or three points (see Tip #20).

Except for its round soundhole, the F-4 model, developed around 1904, had all the features that would become standard in bluegrass mandolins: two scrolls, two points, flat body, teardrop shape, and a carved top and back.

Substitute f-holes for the oval hole (and add a truss rod), and you have the look of the F-5, the most widely imitated bluegrass-style mandolin. It is said to have a crisper, brighter tone than the F-4. There is no doubt that Bill Monroe's use of the F-5 propelled it to mandolin stardom. Many manufacturers imitate its look today. The mandolin pictured in Tip #1 is a typical example.

 # MANDOLIN BANJOS

A mandolin banjo is a mandolin with a banjo head, which gives it a plunky, banjo-like sound. The banjo head is a wooden or metal hoop with a plastic or hide head stretched across and tightened with brackets, like a drumhead. With its eight strings tuned just like a mandolin, the mandolin banjo is played just the same as any other mandolin.

Because the mandolin banjo is louder than its "parent instrument," it was often played in early 20th century string bands as well as mandolin and banjo orchestras. Vega and Gibson manufactured them during that period and—up until recently—they were rarities. Today, several musical instrument companies manufacture and sell them.

RESONATOR MANDOLINS

In the late 1920s, John Dopyera developed a guitar and a mandolin that had an aluminum cone (called a *resonator*) set into the soundboard to increase the instruments' volume. During this period, sound amplification was minimal or non-existent in most musical venues, so resonator (also called *resophonic*) instruments had a distinct advantage, especially in large bands that included horns, drums, and piano. In addition to the extra volume, they have a distinctive, metallic-electric tone.

The earliest resonator mandolins had a round-edged, triangular shape and sometimes the entire instrument was made of metal except for the neck. Later models have the teardrop shape or, less often, the shape of the F model mandolin.

Both the National and the Dobro Manufacturing Companies (originally combined) helped develop resonator mandolins and guitars. Today, many companies manufacture similar instruments.

7 ELECTRIC MANDOLINS

If you peruse vintage photos of country or Western swing bands, you'll often see acoustic mandolins with pickups attached near the bridge or directly over the soundhole. Today, you can install an electric pickup inside an acoustic mandolin or buy one that has a built-in pickup between the bridge and the end of the fretboard. Some will also have volume and tone knobs on the soundboard, just like a hollow body electric guitar. These models are referred to as acoustic-electric mandolins which can be plugged into an amp or PA sound system for extra volume.

In the mid-1950s, both the Gibson and Fender Companies created solid body electric mandolins. A few other companies followed suit and eventually four-string, five-string, and eight-string electric models were developed but many of these models ceased production years ago. However, today, several companies—Blue Star, Kentucky, Stewart-MacDonald, and Rono—are once again producing solid body electrics with four, five, and eight strings. Fender stopped producing their solid body, four-string Mandocaster in 1972, but now they have an almost identical model called the Mandostrat. As you'd expect, it looks like a Stratocaster guitar that stayed in the dryer too long!

Electric mandolins have long been used by blues musicians and in Western swing bands. Instrument manufacturers were selling them as early as the late 1920s. Today, they are used in rock and roots-rock jam bands, or country bands. In fact, many players who favor the acoustic sound when recording may opt for an electric mandolin when performing, just to make sure they are heard!

Tiny Moore—who played with Bob Wills and his Texas Playboys in the 1940s—is the most famous electric mandolin player. He played an electric eight-string Gibson, but strung it with only four strings. In the 1950s, he had Paul Bigsby build a five-string model with a low C string (like a viola). His jazzy style and sound have been much admired and imitated by other pickers.

MANDOCELLO, MANDOBASS, AND MANDOLAS

Mandolin orchestras (see Tip #88) often employ many different size mandolins. These variant models parallel the members of the violin family, both in size and tunings:

- The *mandola* is larger than the mandolin and is tuned C-G-D-A, like a viola. It has eight strings (four courses), like the mandolin.

- The *mandocello*, still larger, is tuned C-G-D-A, like a cello, and sounds an octave lower than the mandola. It also has eight strings (four courses), like the mandolin. Sometimes it is tuned G-D-A-D, like the Irish bouzouki.

- The *mandobass*, even larger still, is tuned E-A-D-G, like a double bass or an electric bass guitar. It has four single strings instead of four courses.

# 9 SCROLLS

The Gibson Company created the scroll for their F model mandolins. Some of Gibson's earliest 1898 mandolins featured a scroll on the mandolin's body and another on the headstock. The 1908 Florentine (F model) sported the ornate scroll shape that became the standard.

There is much argument concerning the acoustic effects, if any, resulting from a scroll on the body of the mandolin. Many argue that it's strictly for looks. It has been called "a $2000 strap-hanger," as most players who own a scrolled mandolin attach one end of the strap to it (see Tip #25). But some luthiers cite arcane reasons (involving air pockets and wood vibration) why scrolls affect the tone of a mandolin. They probably do in some way, but no agreement has been reached on the subject!

10 PICKGUARDS

The earliest pickguards were often a tortoise shell inlay on old roundback mandolins. Today, pickguards are usually made of plastic and are optional. Not all mandolins have them. They are strategically placed where the pick is likely to do the most damage; the wood on the soundboard (See Tip #1).

The carved front and back, F model type mandolins, like many archtop guitars, have a floating pickguard, elevated on metal support brackets. Some are adjustable—they can be raised or lowered—for players who rest their ring and little fingers on the pickguard. The floating pickguard has two other advantages:

1) It's removable. Many players prefer no pickguard at all.

2) It doesn't touch the soundboard. It's widely believed that anything that touches the soundboard diminishes the instrument's sound.

 TAILPIECES

Strings are attached to the tailpiece which is attached to the mandolin's body. Some tailpieces are decorative with elaborate shapes or designs carved into the metal. They may have a removable metal cover plate which hides the rather messy looking string ends. Some cover plates are hinged so that you can open them to change the strings. Others slide right off the tailpiece and get lost if you're not careful where you put them down.

 COURSES

The mandolin has pairs of strings called *courses* just like the twelve-string guitar, the oud, the bouzouki, and many other stringed instruments. On the mandolin, there are four courses with each string pair tuned in unison. This means (starting with the highest pitched strings) you have two E strings (the first course, or first and second strings), two A strings (the second course, or third and fourth strings), two D strings (the third course, or fifth and sixth strings) and two G strings (the fourth course, or seventh and eighth strings).

This can lead to confusion as sometimes the two high E strings are referred to as "the first string," the two A strings are called "the second string," and so on. It's a natural shorthand because the two strings of each course are almost always played at the same time.

String courses help enhance the mandolin's volume. Most of the mandolin's ancestors featured courses too. One variant had sixteen strings arranged in four courses of four strings per course!

13 TUNING

The standard mandolin tuning is (low to high) G-D-A-E; from the fourth to the first course of strings. This tuning is about two centuries old and it duplicates the standard violin tuning with one exception: the violin has only four strings instead of four pairs (courses).

The mandolin and violin are tuned in fifths, which means—starting at the lower string—each subsequent string is a fifth higher. The fourth course on the mandolin is G, and the third course is D, which is a fifth above. The second course is A, which is a fifth above D, and so on.

14 CROSS TUNINGS

When an old-time or bluegrass fiddler tunes differently than G-D-A-E, it's called a *cross tuning*. The most common one is A-E-A-E, which makes fiddle tunes in the key of A easier to play. Mandolin players sometimes use a similar tuning, G-D-G-D, which is easier on the mandolin because you tune two courses down instead of up. Increasing string tension by raising the pitch of several strings can be harmful to the instrument.

The G-D-G-D tuning, also called "open G," makes it easy to play in the key of G. You can play a low G drone on the lowest course while playing melody on the higher strings. That droning sound suits many fiddle tunes. Another advantage of the open G tuning is you can play melody on the top two courses and then duplicate it on the lower two for variety.

Irish folk musician Andy Irvine sometimes plays his mandolin in F-C-G-C tuning, which is a step lower than the G-D-A-D tuning used by Irish bouzouki players. Blues mandolinist Yank Rachell tuned a minor third lower than standard tuning: G-D-A-E dropped down to E-B-C♯-F♯. Jethro Tull used both G-D-G-D and its step-lower twin, F-C-F-C.

15 HARMONIZED COURSES

Some mandolin players have experimented with tunings in which a course (pair) of strings is tuned to two different pitches. For example, when playing the old fiddle tune "Get Up John," Bill Monroe tuned to AF♯-DD-AA-AD so that picking the fourth or first course gave him an automatic harmony. On another Monroe piece, "My Last Days on Earth," he tuned to G♯G♯ -C♯C♯-G♯B-C♯E. Del McCoury's son Ronnie played "Black Mountain Rag" with a variant of the open G cross tuning: GG-DD-GG-BD. The famous Czech mandolinist Radim Zenkl has composed pieces with many complex tunings that include courses tuned to harmonies.

Here's an improvisation in that "Get Up John" tuning. It's reminiscent of the old fiddle tune, "Old Joe Clark."

Get Up Old Joe

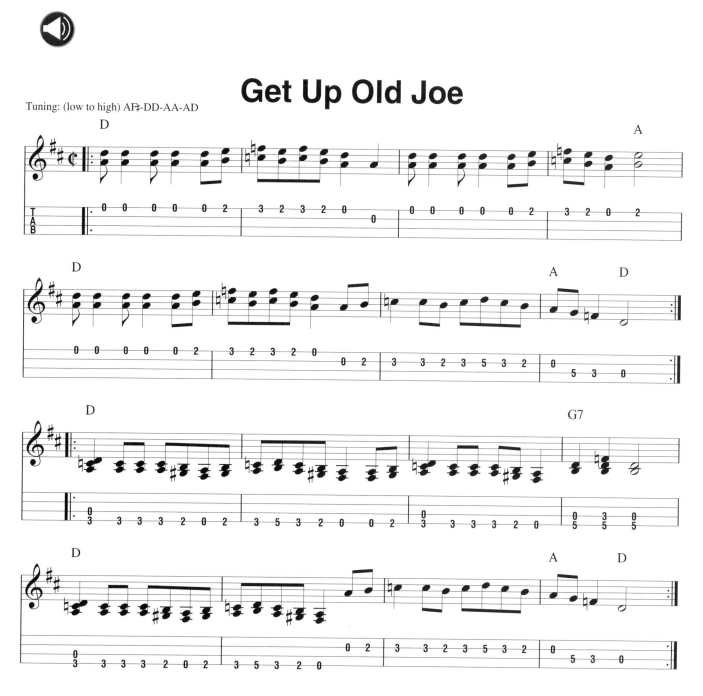

Tuning: (low to high) AF♯-DD-AA-AD

 **ACTION**

The distance between the strings and the fretboard is often referred to as the *action.* High action makes it harder to press down on (fret) the strings, but if the action is too low, the strings will buzz or rattle against the frets when you bear down and pick hard. The trick is to get the action just right for your style of playing.

There are several ways to alter the action:

- If your bridge height is not adjustable (see Tip #19), you can raise the action by switching to a higher bridge or lower it by switching to a lower bridge.

- You can deepen the notches in the nut.

- If your mandolin has a truss rod (see Tip #18), you can adjust the rod to straighten a warped neck which also affects the action.

Consult your neighborhood music store rather than attempt any of these adjustments yourself unless you're willing to do a lot of preliminary research! There are numerous illustrated articles online as well as YouTube videos on the subject.

 **CARE AND MAINTENANCE**

Consider these daily maintenance tips to protect your mandolin:

- After playing, wipe off the strings with a soft cloth to remove sweat or oil left by your fingers. It prolongs the life of the strings. Many string-cleaning products are available as well.

- When you replace the strings, clean the fretboard with a soft cloth. Some people polish the fretboard with almond oil. You can also polish the wood occasionally with a non-silicone, non-wax furniture polish.

- If your mandolin leaves the house, it should be in a case (see Tip #28).

- Extreme heat and cold are bad for wood. Don't leave your mandolin lying in the direct sunlight, next to a heater or in a very cold room, like a basement.

- Don't leave your mandolin in a car, especially the trunk, for more than a few minutes.

- If you live in a climate with extreme weather, you may want to put a humidifier in the mandolin case. Humidifiers are available online or at your local music store.

TRUSS RODS

If your mandolin's neck is warped, or if you have string buzzing that isn't caused by uneven frets or low action, you may need to adjust your *truss rod*...if your mandolin has one! Many mandolins have a metal pole inside the neck that extends the length of the neck. If your instrument has a truss rod, you will see a cover plate on the headstock that conceals an adjusting nut.

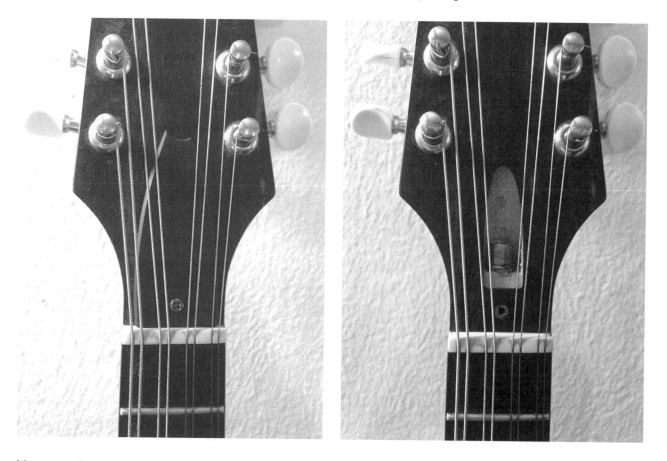

You can alter the curve of the neck by turning the adjusting nut. This will correct high/low action or "warpage" that causes strings to buzz. Online articles or YouTube videos on how to do this may be listed under "mandolin neck relief" or "mandolin setup."

19 BRIDGES

The *bridge* transmits string vibrations to the soundboard and is very important to the mandolin's overall sound. For example, if you touch or pinch the bridge while playing a note, it dampens the sound considerably. Most bridges are made of hardwood and have two metal knobs that allow you to adjust bridge height in order to raise or lower the string action (see Tip #16).

The bridge is not glued to the mandolin's soundboard, but is held on by string pressure alone. So if you remove all the strings at once, the bridge comes off. Here's how to make sure the bridge is placed properly for good intonation (fretted strings giving you the right pitch):

- Play a harmonic (see Tip #46) on the first string at the 12th fret.

- Play the same string fretted at the 12th fret. It should be the same note as the harmonic.

- If the fretted note is sharp (higher in pitch than the harmonic), move the bridge slightly back, toward the tailpiece, until the two notes are identical.

- If the fretted note is flat (lower in pitch than the harmonic), move the bridge forward, away from the tailpiece, until the two notes are identical.

As a mandolin ages, the wood may shrink which causes the bridge to move slightly and therefore affects the intonation. This is called "bridge creep."

20 POINTS

Around 1908, the Gibson Company began making the Florentine, or F-style, mandolin that featured a scroll, a carved front and back (like a violin), and an oval soundhole. This model also featured three decorative points. Very soon after, another model was introduced with two points (the point near the scroll was eliminated), as shown in the illustration for Tip #1. The two-point model was just a few years and a few modifications away from the F-5 that Bill Monroe popularized; a very widely imitated design.

Some players say the two points help them balance the instrument on their lap, but it's likely the design was purely decorative. Whether or not they serve a practical purpose, points appear on mandolins from many manufacturers along with the scroll and other features of the F models.

21 SELECTING A MANDOLIN

Get the best mandolin you can afford. Consider that the better the instrument, the easier it is to play and the quicker you'll improve. Plus, if you're excited about your mandolin every time you open the case, you'll spend more time with it and advance more quickly!

Go someplace where you can try out several different mandolins, and when you do, here's what to look for:

- Is it easy to fret? Does the fingerboard feel comfortable when you fret chords on it?

- Is the neck straight? Look down the neck like you would through a gunsight.

- Is the neck too thick? Some necks are harder to get your hand around than others.

- When you're playing a chord, is the fretboard too narrow for your fingers? Does it have a good sound compared to other mandolins you've played?

- Do you like the way it looks?

- The roundback versus A model or F model issue is not important unless you plan to play professionally in a bluegrass band, in which case, you probably want an F model. Most people find flatback mandolins easier to hold than roundbacks.

- Some entry level mandolins are stripped down (no frills) but have well-made necks and are good for beginners. They don't look like an F-5, but they play well and have good intonation and a decent sound.

22 *PRACTICE WITH A METRONOME*

If you discover that your rhythm is erratic (you get out of synch) while playing with other people or with recordings, practice with a metronome.

A metronome is a mechanical or digital device that keeps time by emitting rhythmic clicks or beeps at variable, measurable speeds. It forces you to keep a steady tempo! You can set your metronome to whatever speed suits you. Musicians have used the metronome for centuries as a practice aid. Its numerical settings are standard throughout the world (beats per minute or "bpm") and are often noted on written music to indicate the preferred tempo of a piece.

If you wander off the beat by speeding up or slowing down, those insistent ticks, tocks, clicks or beeps make it impossible to ignore your error. You can buy inexpensive metronomes and/or there are several free ones online, as well as smartphone apps.

23 GET ORGANIZED

Keep it all together — in a binder: Random scraps of paper won't do! Have a music binder or folder containing all the songs and exercises on which you're working, as well as all the tunes you already know. Add your repertoire list. Carry it with you everywhere you go with the mandolin — to jam sessions, music lessons, the park, friends' houses, etc. Alphabetize the songs, so you can find them easily!

Build up a set list: Make a list of songs you can play all the way through. You're building up a repertoire. Keep the list in your mandolin case. You'll need it at jam sessions and at Carnegie Hall. Your list should include the key in which you like to play and sing each song. It doesn't matter how easy or impressively difficult they are, just list songs you like and can play. Even if you can't play a solo on a song, if you know how it goes and know the chord changes, put it on the list. If you can sing it, so much the better!

Get a music stand: When you're reading tab or music notation from songbooks (to follow the lyrics, the chords, or the music), you need a stand; it beats balancing a book in your lap. Some music stands fold up and are portable, but not as stable as the solid stands. There are also desktop stands.

Most mandolin players favor very heavy-gauge picks that don't bend. Tortoise shell picks, now illegal to sell in most countries, are highly prized by bluegrass players. Many varieties of picks of different shapes, sizes, and materials are available, and it's best to try several of them on your mandolin and see which ones feel the most comfortable and sound the best. Here are some shapes that mandolin players prefer, as well as an illustration of how to hold the pick:

Whether you're sitting or standing, a strap makes it easier to play as your hands don't have to support the mandolin's weight when it's hanging from a strap. Guitar straps are too large so be sure to get a strap made for the mandolin.

- A-model mandolins need a strap that has a hole at one end for the end peg and some kind of laces or apparatus that fits under the strings on the headstock, behind the nut, as shown in the illustration below. Some people prefer to have a strap button put on the underside of the neck near where it meets the body. They use a strap with a hole at either end.

- F-model mandolin straps have a hole at one end for the end peg and laces or a loop at the other end to encircle the scroll. Notice in the illustration below that some people put the strap over their right shoulder while others put it around their neck.

26 AMPLIFYING YOUR MANDOLIN

You get the most natural, amplified mandolin sound by playing into a microphone that's connected to an amplifier or a PA system. This limits your motion as you have to stick right by the microphone — no choreography! Here are some alternative ways to amplify your mandolin:

- Many companies make a miniature mic, which can be mounted on a gooseneck that is attached to your mandolin, pointed right at the sweet spot — the place where the instrument emits the best tone. Some of these mini mics plug into a box on the floor that is a preamp with knobs to adjust tone and volume. Or, you can go wireless…

- Pickups, or transducers, are less expensive and less plagued with feedback problems than mini-mics. The pickups can be mounted on the soundboard or bridge. Some do not require a preamp. But…piezo or magnetic pickups?

- Some say piezo pickups make your tone harsh and have feedback problems. However, they are in wide use, easy to install, convenient, and inexpensive.

- Magnetic pickups are more expensive, but they create less feedback problems and many say they render a more natural sound than piezo.

Obviously, all these systems have pros and cons. Go to your local music store and try some of them out on your mandolin.

27 THERE'S AN APP FOR THAT

Mandolin apps are available for all different gizmos from your smartphone to your tablets. Apps for mandolins abound. Many have chord dictionaries, fretboard configurations, strumming patterns, instruction, songbooks, etc. Tuning apps are especially helpful. Be sure to read reviews as some of them seem to be in a perpetual "beta" stage and are not fully developed.

28 JUST IN CASE (MANDOLIN CASES)

Obviously, you want to protect your mandolin. When purchasing a case consider your lifestyle (traveling around or playing at home), the value of your instrument (monetary and sheer love), and the size and shape of your mandolin. Look for a lot of pockets as well. If you're ordering online, be sure to measure your mandolin.

- **Hard Shell Cases:** The basic ones have a bit of internal padding, a good handle, and back strap; the fanciest have pockets, super padding, adjustable internal and external straps, waterproofing, and scuff-resistant outside edges. Most are made of wood or metal.

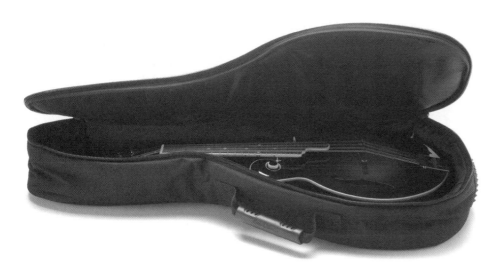

- **Soft Cases/Gig Bags:** More reasonably priced, but not as protective, soft cases are usually made out of heavy-duty (usually waterproofed) and synthetic fabric. The better ones come with dense foam padding. Look for fit, padding, and an industrial-grade plastic zipper that won't scratch your instrument.

29 STRINGS

Many different strings are available from various manufacturers and people often develop a preference for one brand over another. Most importantly, strings vary in thickness.

- **String gauge**: Strings come in different gauges (thicknesses) and your mandolin will sound and feel different depending on what gauge strings you use. String gauges are identified by numbers; for example, the high E strings on a mandolin may be 09 (nine thousands of an inch thick) or 10 or 11. Heavier strings are harder on your fingers, but they usually sound better and sustain (ring out) longer. You need to find the gauge that balances these two factors to your personal satisfaction.

- **String composition**: There are bronze, phosphor bronze, stainless steel, nickel, and many other types of strings. Bronze strings have a brighter sound and stainless steel strings resist sweat. Try different brands and see what feels and sounds best for you.

If you play every day, you'll probably need to change strings every month or so. After a while, they become oxidized and "bent" from being pressed against the frets and will not stay in tune as well, causing bad intonation. When a string breaks, it's usually best to replace the whole set. Be sure to carry an extra set of strings in your mandolin case!

30 MANDOLIN STANDS

When your mandolin is not in its case or in your hands, put it on a stand. It's a safe and handy way to display your instrument at home (see Tip♯ 86). If you're gigging—especially if you're switching back and forth between instruments—you need a safe resting place for the mandolin. No, you do not want to prop it against a chair; that's an accident waiting to happen!

A good stand should be collapsible with an adjustable neck holder, have some sort of locking mechanism, and include a carrying bag.

31 STAY TUNED!

Use an electronic tuner. There are many good, inexpensive models on the market these days. Perhaps the most popular, and easiest to use, clip right onto your headstock. Here are some other varieties.

- **Chromatic Tuners**: Standalone tuners that have all 12 notes of the scale.

- **Pedal Tuners**: Rest on the floor with a microphone wired directly to your mandolin.

- **Pocket Strobe Tuners**: Have a strobe light display rather than a needle to indicate pitch.

- **Apps**: There are also tuning apps available for your smartphone and on websites.

Always pluck the string you're tuning, as you're adjusting its tuning peg, so you can hear when your mandolin is in tune.

If you get a G note from a tuning fork, pitch pipe, piano, or some other instrument that you know is in proper tune, you can use **the time-honored string-to-string method to tune** (used widely before electronic tuners were sold):

- Tune the G(7th and 8th) strings to the tuning fork, piano, or whatever.

- Fret the G strings at the 7th fret. Match the D/6th and 5th strings to this note.

- Fret the D strings at the 7th fret. Match the A/4th and 3rd strings to this note.

- Fret the A strings at the 7th fret. Match the E/2nd and 1st strings to this note.

32 CROSSPICKING

In the 1950s, Jesse McReynolds, the mandolin player in the bluegrass group Jim and Jesse, pioneered a dazzling, rapid flatpicking style that sounds like three-finger, Scruggs-style banjo rolls. Around the same time, George Shuffler, playing with the Stanley Brothers, developed a similar lead guitar flatpicking style. Many bluegrass guitarists and some mandolin pickers have incorporated the picking technique into their music. Some call it *crosspicking*, others call it *McReynolds picking*, honoring Jesse for his unique contribution.

Crosspicking breaks up a bar of 4/4 time into a calypso-like pattern of "two threes and a two," e.g., 1-2-3, 1-2-3, 1-2, or 1-2, 1-2-3, 1-2-3. A different string is plucked on each beat.

Crosspicking Patterns

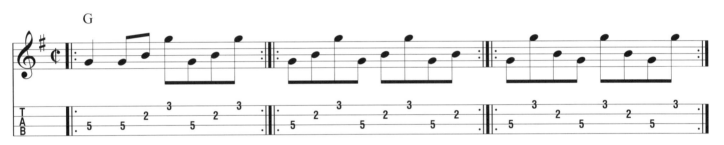

Here's an example of how McReynolds would use these patterns to play the familiar Carter Family tune, "Worried Man Blues."

Worried Man Blues

Not all players use the same pattern of down and up strokes to crosspick. Jesse's roll is "down-up-up, down-up-up, down-up" for one bar of music, whereas Shuffler played "down-down-up, down-down-up, down-up." Other players may strictly alternate down and up strokes as most flatpickers do when playing rapid, eighth-note runs, in spite of the way the crosspicking causes one to skip strings in an odd fashion.

Because of his crosspicking innovation and the split-string technique he popularized (see Tip #33), Jesse McReynolds is considered a major figure in the mandolin world.

33 SPLIT-STRING PLAYING

Frank Wakefield, Jesse McReynolds, and Jethro Burns all experimented with cross tunings. They also employed a *split-string* technique in which you fret single notes within a course. This allows one to play interesting harmonies that are otherwise difficult or impossible to play. Gabriele Leone and other classical mandolin players of earlier centuries used this tricky device in their original compositions (see Tip #90).

On songs like "Dixie Hoedown," McReynolds uses his fingernail to isolate one of the strings in a course. He keeps his left-hand ring fingernail long, with a groove in the middle, to hook the lower string of the E or A courses. The other string in the course may be open or fretted lower than the "hooked" string. Here are some split-string ideas.

Split-string Ideas

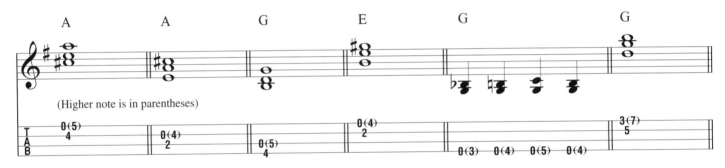

(Higher note is in parentheses)

34 FRETTING HAND MANEUVERS

Usually, you pick strings (and sound notes) with the picking hand. However, the fretting hand also sounds notes by executing *slides*, *hammer-ons*, *pull-offs*, and *bends*.

- A *slide* from one string to another is represented in tab by a line connecting the two frets (the starting and ending points of the slide) and in music notation by a slur. Sometimes you slide up to a fret from one or two frets back, or play a note and then slide down quickly to no specific fret. While sliding, always keep the string firmly pressed down to the fretboard.

- Sometimes you sound a note by striking it suddenly with a fretting finger (instead of plucking it with your picking hand). This is called *hammering on.* You can hammer onto an open string or a fretted string.

- You can sound a note by plucking *down* with your fretting finger. This is called a *pull-off*, which you can do to an open string or a fretted string. You can also pull-off of a string other than the string you just picked. For example, pick the open second string and pull off the first string/2nd fret.

- When you *bend* a note (fret it and stretch it up or down with the fretting finger to raise the pitch), you get a bluesy effect. Mandolin strings are too stiff to bend very much, so this ends up being a subtle effect.

- Here's how all these maneuvers look in tab and how they sound.

Fretting Hand Examples

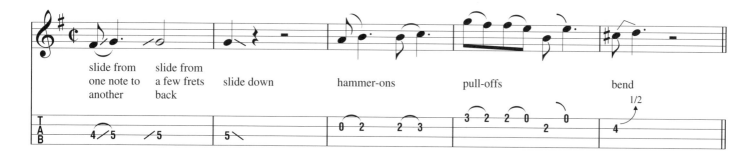

35 FIRST POSITION A MAJOR SCALE

First position means you are playing within the range of the first few frets using some open (unfretted) strings. The keys of A and D are the easiest keys for mandolin, because the A and D major scales include many open strings and "line up" symmetrically on the fretboard. In the A major scale, the fretting pattern on the third and fourth courses is identical to the fretting pattern on the first and second courses.

If you play the A major scale over and over, forwards and backwards, it will get into your fingers' muscle memory and you'll be able to play it without thinking about it. This will make it easier for you to play melodies or solos on the mandolin in the key of A because so many melodies are based on the major scale.

Strum the A chord and then play the A major scale forward and backward.

A Major Scale

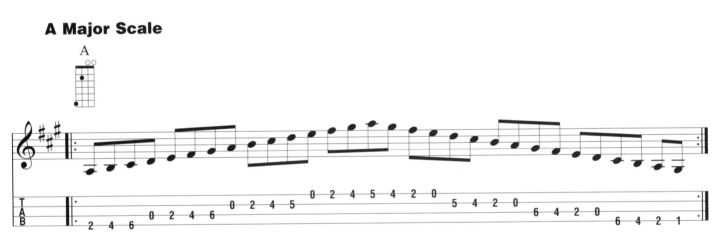

After playing the scale, try picking out melodies to familiar tunes like "When the Saints Go Marching in" and "Clementine" in two different registers—first on the lower strings, then on the higher strings. Listen to the audio and try to pick out the notes by ear.

36 FIRST POSITION D MAJOR SCALE

Strum the D chord and then play the D major scale forward and backward. Notice that the fretting pattern on the second and third courses is identical.

D Major Scale

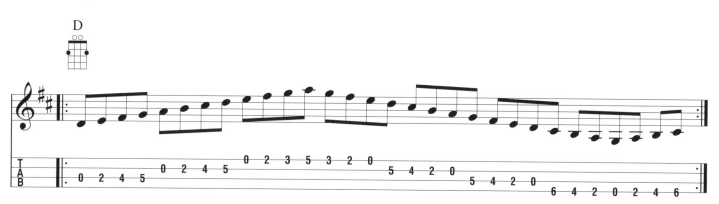

Learn and practice the D major scale and then use it to play "Yankee Doodle," just as we're playing on the recording, in two registers, picking out the notes by ear. Then do the same with "Little Brown Jug." It will only work in one register.

37 FIRST POSITION G MAJOR SCALE

Strum the G chord and then play the G major scale forward and backward.

G Major Scale

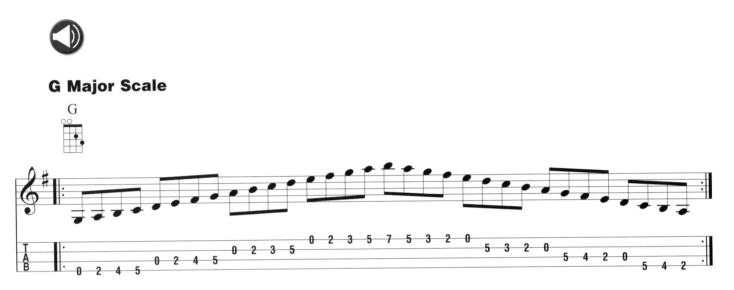

Learn and practice the G major scale and then use it to play "Twinkle, Twinkle Little Star" (hey, it's Mozart!) and "Skip to My Lou" in two registers.

38 FIRST POSITION C MAJOR SCALE

Strum the C chord and then play the C major scale forward and backward.

C Major Scale

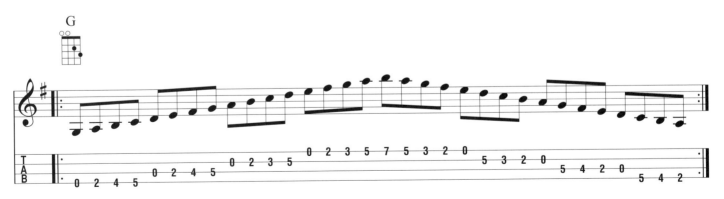

Learn and practice the C major scale and then use it to play "Will the Circle Be Unbroken" and "My Bonnie" in two registers.

FIRST POSITION E MAJOR SCALE

Strum the E chord and then play the E major scale forward and backward.

E Major Scale

Learn and practice the E major scale and then use it to play "Aura Lee" (the same melody as "Love Me Tender") in two registers.

40 PLAY THE BLUES!

The ♭3rd, ♭7th, and ♭5th are *blue notes*, i.e., they're not in the major scale. If you sprinkle them into your ad-lib melody playing, they'll impart a bluesy feel.

Here are the blue notes in the C, G, D, A, and E major scales.

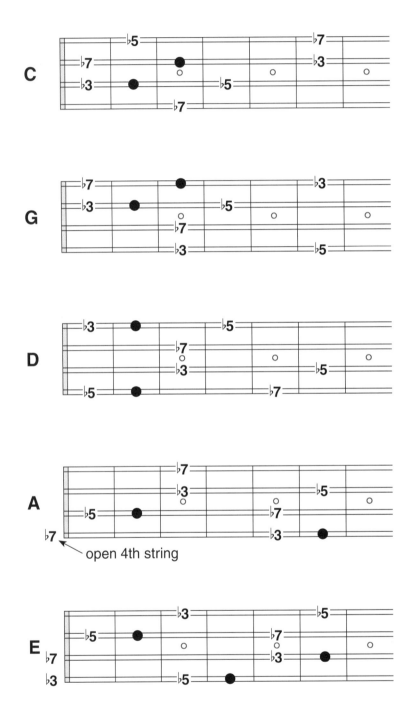

open 4th string

Here's how to "bluesify" a simple melody using the old folk tune, "Nine Pound Hammer." In the notation and tab below, and on the recording, the basic melody is played during the first eight bars. The next eight bars show you how to mix in blue notes.

Nine Pound Hammer

The nine-pound ham-mer   is   a lit-tle too heav-y

for my   size,   bud-dy, for   my   size.

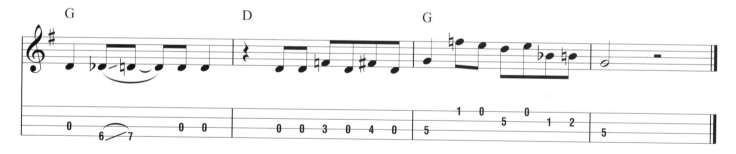

DOUBLE STOPS

Double stop is a violin expression referring to two notes played simultaneously on two different strings. On mandolin, that's *two courses* of strings. Double stops enrich melody playing or accompaniment as they can harmonize your single-note licks.

You can build double stops out of first-position chords.

C Double Stops

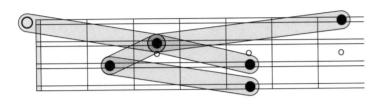

G Double Stops

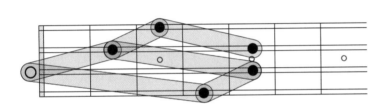

F Double Stops

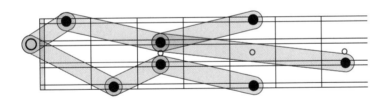

Here's the melody to the old folk tune, "Banks of the Ohio," in the key of C, harmonized with double stops.

Banks of the Ohio

 **CHOP CHORDS**

Bluegrass mandolin players often push the rhythm of a song by playing choppy, staccato *chop chords* on the *backbeats* (the second and fourth beats of each bar). They use chords that have no open strings so they can dampen the strings after the chord is played to get a percussive effect. The dampening is done by lifting your fingers so that they are still touching the strings, but not pressing them against the fretboard. Here's how it sounds.

Nine Pound Hammer

Here are the two most-commonly used chop chords. Notice that you play the C chop chord by moving the G chop chord up a string set.

Chop chords are *moveable,* which means you can use them to play many chords up and down the neck. The D chord in "Nine Pound Hammer" above is the C chop chord shape moved up two frets. Some players include the high first course of strings in the C chop chord shape as shown below.

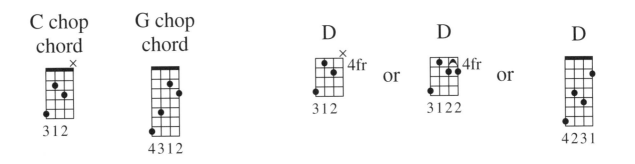

43 ADVANTAGES OF TUNING IN FIFTHS

As mentioned in Tip #13, the mandolin is tuned in fifths: the third string is tuned a fifth (seven frets) above the fourth string; the second string is tuned a fifth above the third string, and so on. See the old string-to-string tuning method shown in Tip #31.

This tuning makes some chords, and partial (two-note) chords, twice or even three times as useful because they can be moved up or down a string. For example, if you move the C chop chord (see Tip #42) up a string, it's a G chop chord.

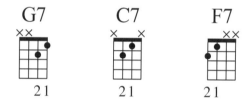

Any two-note chord, played on two adjacent courses, is also moveable.

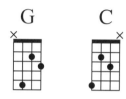

Any lick or scale that doesn't include open strings is also moveable.

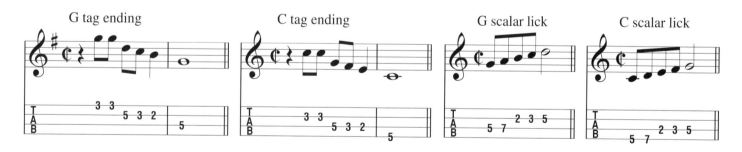

The fact that you can move licks, scales, or chords around this way is an incentive to learn many licks and scales that don't include open strings. Besides moving these musical phrases up and down the fretboard, you can move them up or down a string and use them in any key.

MOVEABLE ASCENDING/ DESCENDING DOUBLE STOPS

Here's an easy double-stop lick that grows out of the first position G and C chords. It harmonizes a little piece of the major scale. Also, notice that the G lick is identical to the C lick moved up a string set.

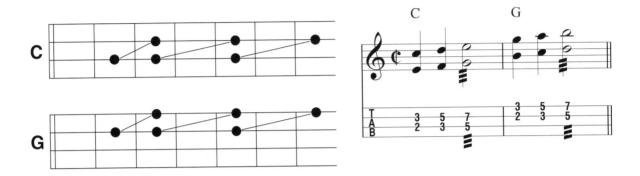

You can use this lick when playing melody or accompaniment and it works well with or without *tremolo* (see Tip #47). Here's an example of the lick as accompaniment to "Down in the Valley," a two-chord song in the key of C. Notice the use of "in-between" double stops.

Down in the Valley

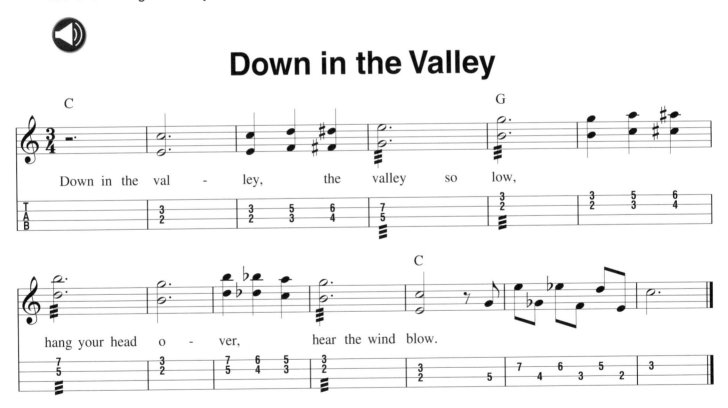

You can base the same double stops on the G and C chop chords, making them moveable and useable in any key. Here's "Down in the Valley," moved up two frets to the key of D.

Down in the Valley – Key of D

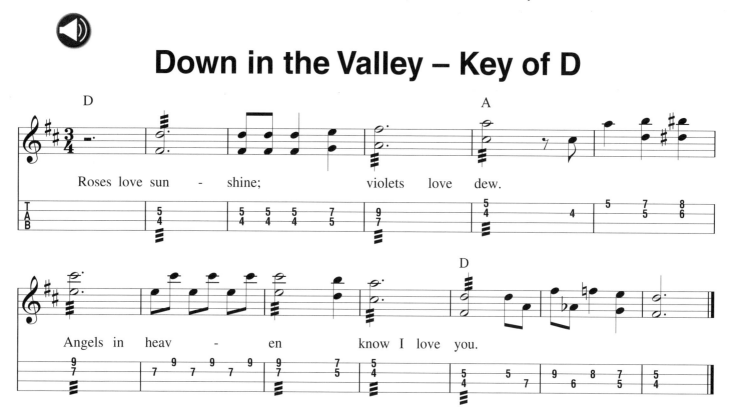

Roses love sun - shine; violets love dew.

Angels in heav - en know I love you.

45 MOVEABLE MAJOR CHORDS

There are other moveable shapes in addition to the chop chords. Here are three moveable major chord shapes, which are *barred* versions of the first position G, C, and D chords. Barring uses a left-hand finger to fret several strings, or courses, at once.

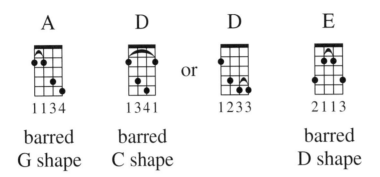

A	D		D	E
1 1 3 4	1 3 4 1	or	1 2 3 3	2 1 1 3
barred G shape	barred C shape			barred D shape

Using these shapes, you can play any major chord three ways.

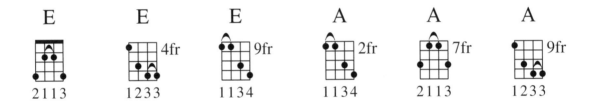

E	E	E	A	A	A
	4fr	9fr	2fr	7fr	9fr
2 1 1 3	1 2 3 3	1 1 3 4	1 1 3 4	2 1 1 3	1 2 3 3

There are moveable major scales that relate to these three chord shapes:

- Before playing one of the major scales, play the related chord shape (barred G, C, or D). *The notes in that chord shape are major scale notes.*

- As you play the scale, you can move your hand off the chord shape to play adjacent major scale notes. Keep coming back to the chord shape as a reference point.

- Play each music/tab scale over and over until you can play it automatically without thinking about it. Each one is a loop that keeps repeating.

- Move each scale up the neck. If you play the barred G/scale at the 2nd fret, it's an A major scale. If you move it up two more frets, it's a B major scale.

- Try picking out some melodies as you did with the first position major scales in Tips #35-39.

E Major Scale

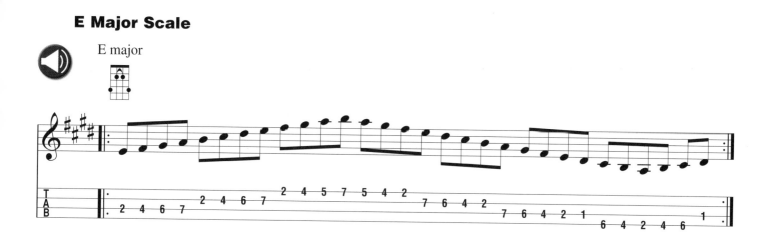

A Major Scale

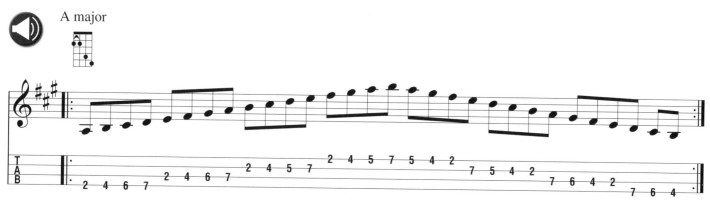

D Major Scale

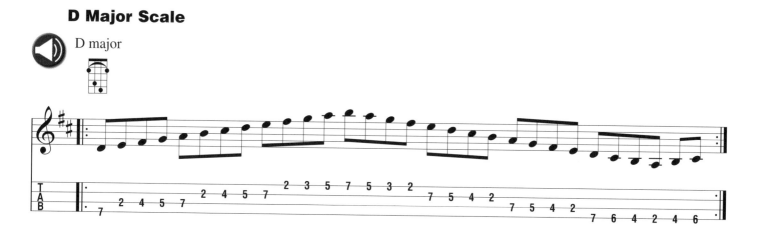

46 HARMONICS!

If you touch a string lightly at certain strategic frets, instead of fretting it the usual way, plucking the string will create a bell-like chime known as a *harmonic*. The easiest place to get harmonics is at the 12th fret; the 7th and 5th frets are the next easiest spots.

- To get harmonics, you have to touch the string (don't push it down to the fretboard) right over the fretwire—not between fretwires as you do when fretting a string.

- To get that bell-like tone, take your fretting finger off the string right after you pluck it.

- The harmonics at the 12th fret are the same notes you get when you fret the strings at the 12th fret; they are an octave higher than the open string.

- Harmonics at the 5th fret are not the same as the fretted notes at the 5th fret. They are the same as the open strings, but two octaves higher.

- Harmonics at the 7th fret are the same notes you get when you fret the strings at the 7th fret, but an octave higher.

- You can strum a whole "chord" harmonic, by barring (but just lightly touching) all four strings at once at the 12th, 7th, or 5th fret.

Physicists know that the strategic harmonic spots on mandolin (or any stringed instrument) are not random. The 12th fret is halfway between the nut and the bridge; the 5th fret is a fourth of the way; and the 7th fret is a third of the way up the neck.

Harmonics can be played on any stringed instrument; they've been used as a pretty effect for centuries in music of all types. You can also use them to tune your mandolin if you can get a starting G note from a tuning fork or pitch pipe or another instrument. Here's how:

- Play a harmonic on the fourth string at the 7th fret.

- Compare this note to the third string harmonic at the 12th fret. They should be identical

- Compare the third string/7th fret harmonic to the second string/12th fret harmonic. They should be identical.

- Compare the second string/7th fret harmonic to the first string/12th fret harmonic. They should be identical.

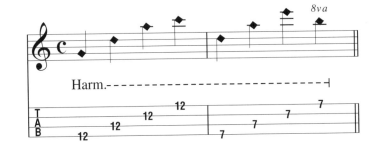

47 TREMOLO

Tremolo is the rapid up-and-down picking on one or more courses of strings, which enables you to sustain a note (or chord) on the mandolin. It is the trademark sound of the instrument, and is used in classical music, bluegrass, country, blues, rock, Italian, and just about every other musical genre.

Here are some tremolo tips from the pros:

- Keep a loose wrist. The tremolo motion comes from the wrist, not the arm or the pick.

- Play with a heavy, unbending pick.

- Rest the palm of your hand, where it meets the wrist, on the strings between the bridge and the tailpiece.

- Start the up-and-down motion slowly, on one course of strings, and gradually increase speed.

- Once you can play a tremolo on one course, try it on two or more.

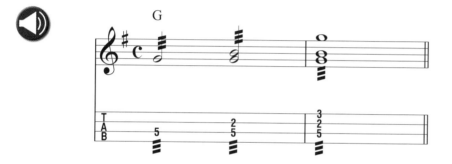

In Italian and classical music, the mandolin often plays chords and melody at the same time. This makes the mandolin a self-contained instrument like a piano or a guitar. The technique, called *chord-melody playing,* or *chord soloing,* can be used in any musical genre. Here are some tips to keep in mind for chord soloing:

- You don't have to play a chord with each melody note; play just enough chords to make the arrangement sound full. One chord per measure may be enough.

- The melody note will stand out if it's the highest note in the chord. For example, if you're playing a first position G chord and the B note on the second string/2nd fret is the melody note, don't play the first string. Just play the fourth, third, and second courses.

- There are many ways to play any chord on the mandolin. Choose the chord shape that includes the melody note. It may be in the first few frets, with open strings, or it may be up the neck at the 7th fret. This means you need to know several *inversions* of any chord!

Here's a simple chord solo arrangement of the old folk hymn, "Amazing Grace," in the key of A.

Amazing Grace

48

A major chord consists of three notes: the first, third, and fifth intervals of the major scale. For example, a C major chord consists of C, E, and G; the first, third, and fifth notes of the C major scale. A minor chord consists of the first, flatted third, and fifth intervals. C minor is C, E♭, and G. Flatting the third makes the sunny, bright major chord sound melancholy.

By shifting one or two fingers around, you can make the moveable major chords (the barred G, C, and D shapes) into minor chords.

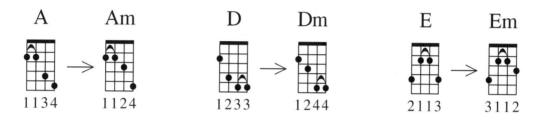

This gives you three ways to play any minor chord:

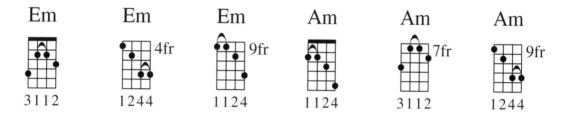

A seventh chord is a major chord with a flatted seventh added. For example, a C7 consists of C, E, G, and B♭; the first, third, fifth, and flatted seventh notes of the C major scale. Seventh chords sound bluesy and have some tension, unlike the "complete" or "at rest" sound of a major chord.

It only takes a slight shift to make any moveable major chord a seventh chord:

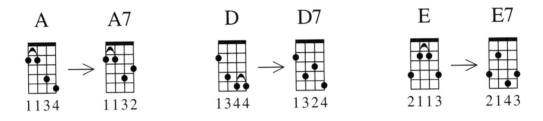

This gives you three ways to play any seventh chord:

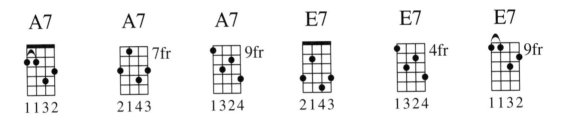

51 PLAY WITH THE BEST BACKUP BANDS IN THE WORLD

Playing along with recorded music is an excellent way to practice. It's the next best thing to playing with other people and it forces you into the rhythm groove and keeps you there. They don't have to be mandolin recordings. You can just choose some familiar songs you like and can play along with. Here are some helpful tips:

- You have to know the song's key. (See Tip #66.)

- You have to know the chord changes. Often, you can find them online or in songbooks. (If they're in a different key than your recording, see Tip #81 on transposing.)

52 LEARN COMPLETE SONGS

If you can play and sing a song from start to finish, you can lead other players in a jam session, serenade your significant other, sing your kids to sleep, enter competitions/talent shows/recitals, annoy your neighbors, or launch your career. This means you'll have to:

- Memorize the words and the chord progression.

- Learn to play/sing the song without reading it!

- Practice a song by *playing it all the way through, over and over.* Don't stop every time you make a mistake and start over again. Just keep playing and try to get it right the next time around.

- If one chord change in a song always trips you up, isolate that section and practice it separately.

It is very helpful to listen to a recording of a song you're trying to learn (by a performer you like) and sing and/or play along, over and over. Periodically, turn off the recording and perform the song by yourself. You'll discover the parts you tend to forget and you can work on those specifically.

53 KEEP A STEADY TEMPO

Most people have a tendency to speed up during the easy parts of a tune and slow down for the hard parts. Not only is this unmusical sounding, it's bad practice!

- Keep to one steady tempo.

- Slow the whole song down to the tempo that allows you to keep a consistent beat. You can speed up gradually once you've ironed out the rough spots.

- Use a metronome (see Tip #22).

54 REPETITION GETS IT DONE

If a new chord, scale, lick, or anything else you're trying to play is difficult at first, repeat it over and over, keeping a steady tempo. The great Indian master musician, Ali Akbar Khan, used to say (after teaching a student something new), "Now play it a hundred times." Eventually, the lick or scale becomes automatic and feels natural. Practice a new chord in the context of a tune, or just switch from a familiar chord to a new one, in tempo.

55 MAKE A WISH LIST (OF SONGS)

List the songs you'd like to learn to play and sing. This can include your all-time favorites—even the ones you may think are too difficult. As you learn them and check them off, you'll add them to your repertoire list (Tip #23). This is a good way to make sure you keep growing as a player.

56 ORGANIZE YOUR PRACTICE

Practice at the same time every day, whenever it's convenient—in the morning before breakfast, at a lunch break, or when you first come home from work. Even if it's only for ten or fifteen minutes a day, daily practice does more for you than one two-hour session a week. You're building physical skills and neural pathways. And just as with athletics, music requires daily exercise; you can't cram (like for a test) at the end of the week. Here are some ideas on how to maximize your practicing time:

- Play the tunes you already know once through, to warm up.

- Play the tunes you're currently working on.

- Practice some scales or common chord changes, using moveable chords. (See Tips #42, 45, 49, and 50 for chords, and #35-39 for scales.)

- Play randomly; discover something new on your mandolin.

57 PRACTICE MENTALLY

You can practice without a mandolin. If you're waiting in a line, on hold on the phone, or on a treadmill, you can visualize the mandolin and go through songs, strumming chords or picking, mentally. Picture exactly where your fingers go and how the strumming or picking works. Visualizing all the movements reinforces patterns.

58 PRACTICE READING

If you read music or tab, practice playing melodies that are written in music books or sheet music. This can include mandolin books, or any kind of music books. "Fake books" are useful and afford great reading practice. They include a single-note melody line in standard music notation, plus chord letter-names and lyrics. If you've heard a tune and want to learn the chords, try playing from a fake book.

In group jams, often you'll be given a lyric sheet with chord letter-names over the lyrics. Beginning with a tune you have already heard, try to sing and strum along following this kind of chart.

59 RECORD YOURSELF

You can record yourself with your computer, an iPhone/smartphone, or all kinds of inexpensive recording devices. You'll hear problems in your playing that you didn't know were there, but you may hear good things as well. Record yourself playing an entire tune from start to finish. Don't be discouraged if what you hear isn't perfect! Once you've spotted a flaw, whether it's a wrong note or irregular timing, work on it and re-record until it sounds better.

60 ONE NEW CHORD AND ONE NEW SONG A WEEK

If you learn just one chord a week, you'll have 52 new chords by the end of the year. You can find new chords in the *Hal Leonard Mandolin Chord Finder*. Make sure you use your weekly new chord in a song. Find a chord chart for a song you've heard before, and if it includes one or two new chord shapes, learn to play it! When you can play a new chord in a song and get to it in time, you own it, and you'll be able to play it in any song. It's part of your vocabulary.

Learn a new song every week, and learn to play it from start to finish. This may mean learning a mandolin solo, an instrumental version of the song, or it may mean learning to back yourself up (playing accompaniment) when you sing the song. Either way, by the end of the year you'll have a sizable repertoire.

This is not as big of a challenge as it sounds. Thousands of well-known songs contain only two or three chords. You grew up hearing and singing many of them ("This Land Is Your Land," "Happy Birthday," "You Are My Sunshine," etc.), and it's fairly easy to learn to strum the chord changes or pick out a melody on your mandolin.

61 EXPAND MANDOLIN CONSCIOUSNESS

Get outside your usual bag; it'll broaden your musical horizons. If you only play bluegrass songs, learn an old-time tune, or vice-versa. For a bigger stretch, learn to strum chords or pick accompaniment to a new pop tune. If you've never played a jazz tune or a reggae tune, learn one. Learn a country standard (accompaniment, solo, or both). You'll find the chords in many songbooks. Here are a few suggestions for classic tunes of their genre:

Country:	"I'm So Lonesome I Could Cry"
Reggae:	"Three Little Birds"
Jazz:	"Georgia on My Mind"
Blues:	Stormy Monday"
Bluegrass:	"Salty Dog Blues"
Old Time:	"Way Down the Old Plank Road"
Classic Rock:	"Stand By Me"
Swing:	"Fly Me to the Moon"
Rockabilly:	"It's So Easy to Fall in Love"
Tin Pan Alley:	"There'll Be Some Changes Made"
Hawaiian:	"Sweet Leilani"
Grunge:	"Come as You Are"
Indie Rock:	"Miss Misery"
Italian:	"Come Back to Sorrento"

62 GET READY FOR SHOWTIME!

If you tell people you play mandolin, they'll say, "Play me something!" (That's if they don't say, "What's a mandolin?") Get a song up to performance level so that you'll be able to play it for them, or perform it at an open mic event. Enter it in a competition or put it up on YouTube. Conquer your stage fright and do one of those things! The threat of public scrutiny will make you work harder at really perfecting a tune—even if your "public" is one or two people in a living room.

To get a tune ready for performance, play it over and over, from start to finish. Don't stop for mistakes, just repeat it and get it right next time. Choose a song that's easy for you to play and sing—one that you're comfortable with.

63 PRACTICE IN FRONT OF A TV

Many pros practice scales, licks, chord changes, strums, picking patterns, or anything that requires mindless repetition and muscle memory, while sitting in front of a *silent* TV. Your favorite nature programs are a good bet for this one. Anything that occupies your mind will do, because the mind just gets in the way.

64 YOU CAN PLAY ANYTHING

If a mandolin arrangement is written out in tab (or music notation, if you read it), you can learn to play it, no matter how difficult it may seem. All you have to do is break it down into short musical phrases and learn them, one at a time, by repeating each phrase over and over, until your fingers "get it." Start by playing each phrase with a slow enough tempo that you can play it with the right rhythmic feel; then gradually speed up.

65 PLAY FIDDLE TUNES

Fiddle tunes fit well on the mandolin because the two instruments are tuned the same way. Many of the fiddle tunes played by old-time or bluegrass pickers are in the keys of A or D because the A and D major scales include so many open strings, making those the easiest keys for playing melodies

Even if bluegrass or old-time music is not your passion, fiddle tunes are great practice exercises. They are usually based on major scales, so when you learn a fiddle tune you are becoming familiar with a major scale in a very natural, non-academic way.

- Most old fiddle tunes have a traditional key. If you ever plan to play music with other people, learn the tunes in the "dedicated" key.

- On the other hand, once you've learned a fiddle tune, try playing it in different keys, as a form of major scale exercise.

Many old fiddle tunes in the old-time and bluegrass repertoire come from the British Isles. Most of them have two sections—each of which is repeated—giving you the form: AABB. Once you play the first section twice and the second section twice, you've gone around the tune once. After that, the next instrument (fiddle, banjo, guitar, etc.) does the same thing as you repeat the tune over and over. Old timers use to call the two sections the "coarse" and the "fine."

Here's an example of an AABB form in one of the more popular fiddle tunes, "Arkansas Traveler."

Arkansas Traveler

66 WHAT KEY ARE WE IN?

A *key* is like a sonic home base. For example, if you're in the key of C, the song's melody is most likely based on a C major scale and feels "at rest" when you play the C chord. Playing any other chord causes tension, which is resolved by coming back to the C.

Here are some tips on how to figure out a song's key by listening (something you need to do in order to play along with a recording, as in Tip #51):

- The key chord is not always the first chord in the song, but it usually is the last chord.

- If a song fades out (so there's no final chord), listen for the resolving chord, the chord on which you *could* end the song.

- Play a G or C chop chord and move it up the neck until you match the resolving chord.

67 VIOLIN/FIDDLE PLAYERS HAVE A HEAD START

The mandolin and violin tunings and fingerings are identical, so if you play fiddle or violin, you already know more than a little about the mandolin. The two instruments share the same scales as well as double stops (playing two strings at once that harmonize with each other). If you've learned fiddle tunes on the violin, you can translate them to mandolin almost automatically. you've got the fretting hand already; you main challenge is using a flatpick instead of a bow.

68 TABLATURE

Also called *tab* for short, tablature is very popular among players of stringed/fretted instruments, because a beginner can learn to read it almost immediately. Tablature has been around since the Renaissance. Unlike standard music notation, tab tells the player which string to pluck and where to fret the string. Today, most mandolin music is written in music and tab, or just tab.

- The four lines of mandolin tablature represent the four courses of strings. The bottom line is the fourth course (strings 8 and 7) and the top line is the first course (strings 2 and 1); it's as if you looked down at the fretboard while holding the mandolin in playing position.

- Numbers on the lines represent frets. For example, a 3 on the top line tells you to play the first string at the 3rd fret.

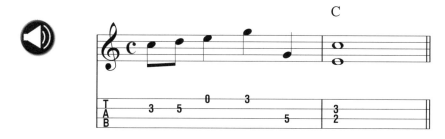

69 UP AND DOWN

"Up" is toward the bridge; "down" is toward the nut. Why? As you move up a string toward the bridge, you raise the pitch; when you move down a string, toward the nut, you lower the pitch. So, if you're playing a G chop chord and you're told to "move it up two frets to play an A," move it toward the bridge.

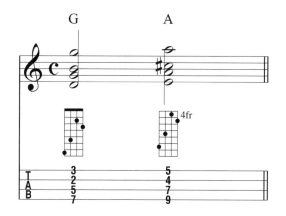

70 WHERE THE NOTES ARE

You can play mandolin all your life without knowing the names of the notes you're playing. Pete Seeger often quoted an old gag where a fellow asks the mandolin player, "Do you read music?" And he responds, "Not enough to hurt my playing." Though most mandolin styles heard today are part of an aural tradition, there are many situations in which it would be helpful to know how to read music, or at least know where the notes are. This chart shows the note positions:

- Notice the spaces between many of the notes, with no letters (for example, the space between C and D on the second string). These are *sharps* and *flats*.

- *Sharp* means "a fret higher." C♯ (C sharp) is one fret above C.

- *Flat* means "a fret lower." D♭ (D flat) is one fret below D.

- Each of these "in-between" notes has two names. The note between C and D can be called C♯ or D♭.

- Notice that there are sharps or flats between most of the letter names (notes), but there is no sharp or flat between B and C or E and F.

Start by learning the notes in the first four or five frets, and your knowledge of notes on the fretboard will creep up the neck gradually as you continue to play.

71 TWO FRETS BETWEEN MOST NOTES

Most of the letter-names (G, A, B, etc.) are two frets apart as the diagram below shows:

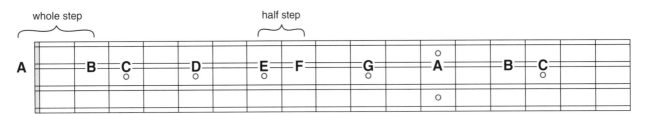

There are two exceptions: B and C are only one fret apart (there is no B♯ or C♭) and likewise, E and F are only one fret apart (there is no E♯ or F♭).

Two frets apart is called a *whole step* and one fret is apart is called a *half step.*

72 SHARPS AND FLATS

- Notice while moving the G chop chord up the neck (Tip #42) one fret, you "sharp" the chord and it becomes a G♯ chord. Notes are also "sharped" when you raise them one fret.

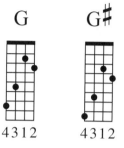

- You "flat" a note or chord by moving it down a fret.

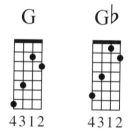

- Sharp or flat notes (or chords) can have two names. The note between F and G can be called F♯ or G♭. The G chord, moved up a fret, can be called G♯ or A♭ (the A note moved down one fret).

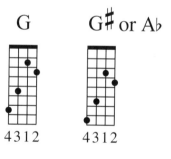

73 DIMINISHED CHORDS REPEAT

A diminished chord is a seventh chord (1, 3, 5, ♭7) with everything flatted but the root (1). The resulting formula for a diminished chord is 1, ♭3, ♭5, and 6.

Move a diminished chord up three frets and you have the same chord with a different voicing (the same notes are stacked up in a different order). You can keep moving it up three frets until you run out of frets and it's always the same chord:

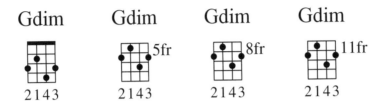

Knowing this fact, you can play fancy licks every time a diminished chord occurs in a song by sliding it up or down the neck. Listen to Track 26 to hear an example.

Diminished Chord Lick

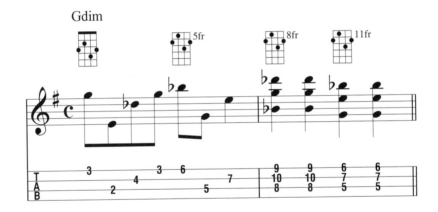

A diminished chord is composed of four notes and it can be named after any of the four.

Gdim, D♭dim, Edim, B♭dim

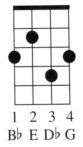

1 2 3 4
B♭ E D♭ G

74 AUGMENTED CHORDS REPEAT, TOO

An augmented chord is a major chord with a ♯5th. The resulting formula is: 1, 3, ♯5. So, for example, a C augmented chord is spelled: C, E, G♯.

Move an augmented chord up four frets and you have the same chord with a different voicing. You can keep moving it up four frets until you run out of frets and it's always the same chord.

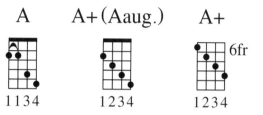

Listen to the Track 27 for some uses of the moveable augmented chord.

Augmented Chord Lick

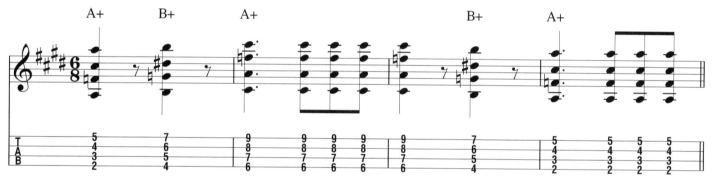

75 USING SEVENTH CHORDS

As mentioned in Tip #50, seventh chords have tension while major chords feel at rest. This tension is usually resolved by playing the chord that is a 4th higher. For instance, G7 leads to C, C7 leads to F, and so on. Play any seventh chord, followed by the major chord that is a 4th higher, and listen to the feeling of resolution it brings.

You can use seventh chords to "lead up a 4th." If you're playing a G chord followed by a C chord, play a G7 before the C to give it a push in that direction. Try it and see!

76 THE BLUES LOVES 7TH CHORDS

The rule in Tip #75 doesn't apply to the blues. In the blues, you often use seventh chords throughout instead of major chords, and they don't necessarily lead up a 4th. You can even end a blues tune on a seventh chord.

77 THE NUMBERS GAME

Musicians, pro and amateur, often use numbers rather than letters to name chords. At jam sessions, folks are just as likely to call out numbers ("go to the 4 chord") as letters ("go to the F chord").

The numbers refer to steps of the major scale of a song's key. For example, in the key of C, a C chord is called the 1 chord. The second note in the C major scale is D, so if you're playing in the key of C, a D chord is called a 2 chord — whether it's a D, Dm, D7, or any variation of D.

- Whatever key you're in, 1, 4, and 5 are the chords most often played. Countless blues, rock, country, folk, and bluegrass tunes use just these three chords.

- Use the "Circle-of-Fifths" chart (Tip #79) to identify the 1, 4, and 5 chords in any key, and become familiar with these "immediate chord families."

- You can become familiar with the *sound* of the 4 chord or the 5 chord in relationship to the 1 chord. When you do, you're starting to understand the basis of music theory. You're figuring out how music works! Here's how to train your ear: take a simple, three-chord song that just contains the 1, 4, and 5 chords and write numbers under the letters. For example:

When the Saints Go Marching In

C			G7
Oh, when the saints	go marching in,	oh when the saints go marching in,	
1			5

G7	C	F	C	G7 C
oh Lord, I want to be in that number, when the saints go marching in.				
5	1	4	1	5 1

Play the song several times, being aware that when you change to G7, you're going to the 5 chord, and when you change to F, it's the 4 chord. Use the "Circle-of-Fifths" chart (Tip #79) to play the song in several different keys. (See Tip #81 on Transposing.) Whatever key you're in, be aware when you're going to the 4 chord or the 5 chord.

It's helpful to know what 1, 4, and 5 are in any key, without having to stop and think about it. The following chart shows you what they are in several easy mandolin keys:

1-4-5 Chord Family Chart

	1	4	5
Key of E	E	A	B
Key of A	A	D	E
Key of D	D	G	A
Key of G	G	C	D
Key of C	C	F	G
Key of F	F	B♭	C
Key of B♭	B♭	E♭	F

78 1-4-5 CHOP CHORD FAMILIES

Tip #42 mentions that when you move a C chop chord up a string set, it becomes a G chop chord.

Going from a C chord to a G chord is "moving up a fifth," since G is the fifth note in the C major scale. This is true anywhere on the fretboard. If you play a C chop chord at any fret, move it up a string to play its 5 chord:

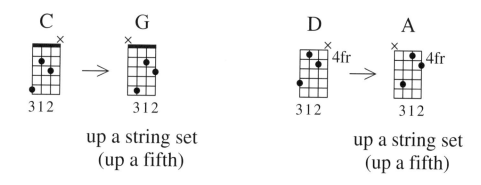

up a string set
(up a fifth)   up a string set
(up a fifth)

Moving in the opposite direction—down a string set—is "moving up a fourth":

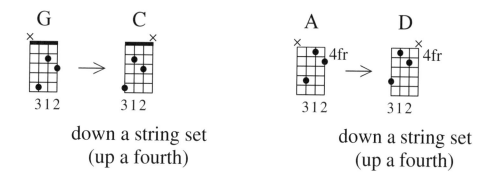

down a string set
(up a fourth)   down a string set
(up a fourth)

The resulting 1-4-5 chop chord relationships make it easy to find chord families in any key:

- If the 1 chord is a C chop chord, move up a string set to find the 5 chord (the G chop chord at the same frets), then Move the 5 chord down two frets to find the 4 chord.

- If the 1 chord is a G chop chord, move down a string set to find the 4 chord (the C chop chord at the same frets), then move the 4 chord up two frets to find the 5 chord.

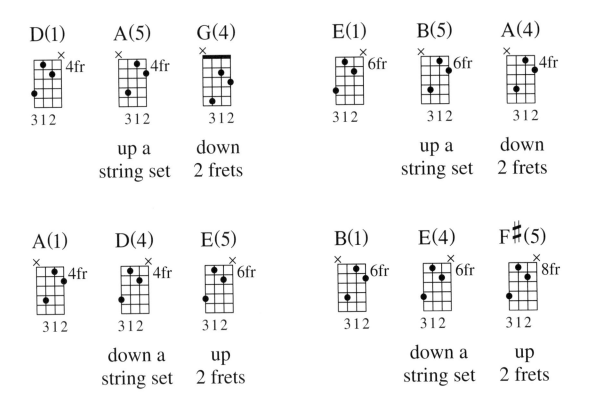

Strum the following 1-4-5-4 progression using chop chord families, in several keys starting with the three keys of Track #29. It's the classic rock progression of many tunes such as "Louie, Louie," "Wild Thing," and "Twist and Shout."

Classic Rock Progression

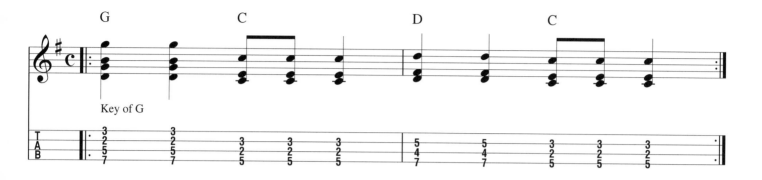

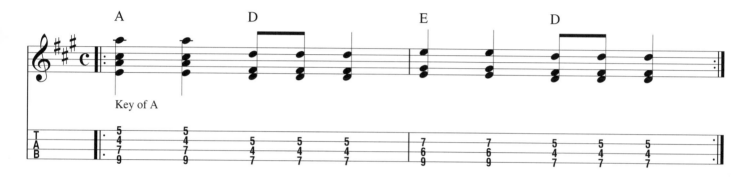

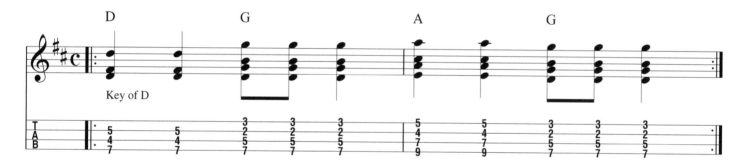

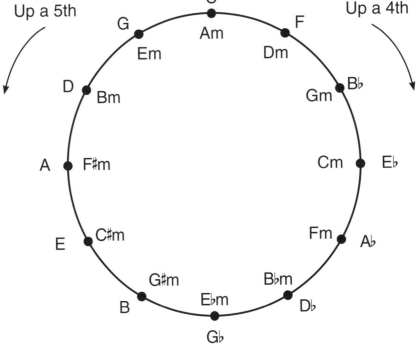

This chart groups chords in their 1-4-5 chord families. For example, if you look at the C at the top of the chart, the note (or chord) that's a 4th above C is one step clockwise. The note (or chord) a 5th above C is one step counter-clockwise.

The same applies in any key. The chart says that, if you're in the key of E, the 4 chord is A (one step clockwise), and the 5 chord is B (one step counter-clockwise). Many songs have circle-of-fifths-type chord movement. For example, many songs start on the 1 chord and jump outside the chord family to a chord that is several steps counter-clockwise. Then they go clockwise, up by 4ths, to get back to the 1 chord. A song in the key of C may have this chord progression:

    | C | A7 | D7 G7 | C ||

In this chord progression, you jump several steps counter-clockwise from C (the 1 chord) to A7. Then, using typical circle-of-fifths movement, you go clockwise (up a 4th) from A7 to D7, then up another 4th to G7, and up still another 4th to end back at C.

The chords inside the circle are *relative minors* (see Tip #80).

80 A RELATIVELY MINOR PROBLEM

Every major chord has a *relative minor,* a closely related minor chord that is built on the sixth note of the major chord's scale. For example, the sixth note in the C major scale is A, so Am is the relative minor of C.

- Many songs include the relative minors of the 1 chord, the 4 chord, or the 5 chord — or any combination of them.

- Listen to the sound of a relative minor when it's played after the relative major chord. You've heard that chord change in a lot of popular songs, and now you can recognize it when you next hear it.

- Play a C, and follow it with an Am. Do the same with a G and Em, and a D and Bm. Notice the similarities: no matter what key you're in, going from a major chord to its relative minor has an unmistakable sound.

- A shortcut: The relative minor is also three frets below the relative major. For instance, to find the relative minor of D, go three frets down from D (D♭, C, B); Bm is the relative minor of D.

Knowing how to locate a relative minor chord can immediately come in handy. Here's how you change each of the moveable major chord shapes into their relative minors:

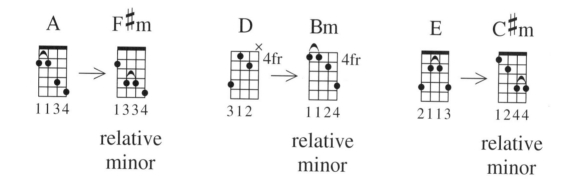

81 TRANSPOSING

Transposing simply means changing keys. If a song you'd like to sing is written in a key that's too high or too low for your voice, you can transpose it to whatever key you like. You can change all the chords using the Circle-of-Fifths chart (Tip #79).

For example, if the song is written in D, and you can't quite reach the high notes, transpose it a whole step lower to the key of C. C is two steps clockwise from D on the circle, so all the chords in the tune must be changed two steps clockwise.

82 FIND A PICKING PARTNER!

Once you've learned a handful of chords and some strums, it's time to find a musically like-minded jam partner. Playing music with another player is fun and it adds a whole new dimension to your mandolin experience.

- Your playing partner(s) could play anything: piano, guitar, sax, accordion, or drums. You name it!

- Playing with others exposes your weaknesses and strengths. They might call out a chord you don't know, or play in keys that are difficult for you. You may discover your rhythm is erratic, or that it's really strong.

- If you have a friend who plays guitar, piano, or anything at all, arrange a weekly get-together and build up a repertoire of songs you can play.

No matter what your musical genre, you can find a jamming partner with a common interest. Ask your friends, family, and co-workers about other players. When you get together with them, have some songs in mind that you can play well. Try to find some tunes you all know and be open to learning new ones. It's a one-of-a-kind experience!

83 FIND A JAM GROUP

Take Tip #82 a step farther and find a jam group! You'll be amazed how much fun it is to get into a solid rhythmic groove with a bunch of pickers. And, it's the fastest way to progress as a player.

There are free bluegrass, blues, old-time, and folk music jams meeting on a regular basis at private homes, music stores, restaurants, or clubs that have live entertainment. Most jam groups are non-competitive, supportive, and non-threatening. A typical format is to sit in a circle and sing or play a tune together, taking turns soloing. When it's your turn to solo, you can decline. Some people never solo in a jam session and just play backup while others relish the opportunity to play solos.

Come to a jam with an open mind and a list of tunes you know, and don't worry about playing imperfectly or making mistakes. You're bound to learn something from just about every player with whom you jam and that can be inspiring!

84 DIFFERENT TEACHERS

Try out several teachers; each has a different approach and will give you different ideas. These could be flesh-and-blood teachers in your neighborhood music store, instructional books, or cyber-teachers on the web. There are tons of instructional YouTube videos, for example. Try out as many as you can until you find an approach that suits your learning style best.

85 LOOK, LISTEN, AND LEARN

Listen to a lot of mandolin players! And watch them in person and online. You'll see and hear new playing styles or techniques, you'll find new inspiration, and you'll discover new songs you want to learn. When there's a bluegrass or old-time band, mandolin orchestra or folk musicians performing in your neighborhood, make it a point to go see them.

86 LEAVE IT OUT— AT ARM'S LENGTH!

A mandolin that's hanging on the wall, sitting on the couch, or resting on a stand in the living room or den will get played more often than the mandolin that's locked up in a case. You'll progress more as a result. However, do take into consideration heat, cold, humidity (or lack thereof), earthquakes, and the worth of the instrument!

87 VISIT MANDOLIN WEBSITES

There are many good mandolin websites, which often include blogs and discussions about everything related to mandolin. Many of them announce mandolin performances, seminars, classes, and other mandolin-related events. They may also help you find jamming groups or partners in your area. One website often links to many others, but just for starters, look up:

Mandolincafe.com, jazzmando.com, emando.com (for electric mandolin players), **mandolinmagazine.com, classicalmandolinsociety.org,** and **mandohangout.com**

 88 MANDOLIN ORCHESTRAS

Mandolin orchestras have been around for decades and new ones are popping up constantly. According to **www.classicalmandolinsociety.org**, there are over seventy mandolin orchestras across the U.S., plus a number in Canada and Europe. See if you can find one that performs in your neighborhood!

Mandolin orchestras may include guitars and any combination of mandocellos, mandolas, mandolin banjos, and mandobasses. Though they primarily play classical music, several orchestras draw their repertoire from other genres too.

Have a look and a listen at the classical mandolin scores and mandolin music clips featured on the website. If you like what you see and hear—and if your music reading skills are up to it—join a mandolin orchestra!

 89 FESTIVALS AND CAMPS

There are annual old-time and bluegrass festivals occurring globally throughout the year. Some feature local and well-known, world-class performers. They often have workshops and instruction as well. Just type in "Bluegrass Festivals" or "Old-Time Festivals" into your search engine and plan your next vacation.

Music camps, like the Kaufman Akoustic Kamp, employ well-known instructors to conduct classes in mandolin and other instruments. Some camps last a weekend, others a whole week. These are exciting and inspiring events and are often held in beautiful areas, so they're somewhat like a musical retreat. You're surrounded by other fans of the music you like too, so they're always an enjoyable learning experience.

Here are a few camps from **www.mandolincafe.com**:

- The American Mandolin & Guitar Summer School

- Camp Bluegrass

- Classical Mandolin Society of America (they have an annual convention)

- Cape Cod Mandolin Camp

- Mandolin Camp North

- Steve Kaufman's Acoustic Mandolin Camp

- NashCamp

90 KNOW YOUR MANDOLIN MASTERS PAST

Bluegrass and Country

- Bill Monroe: Father of bluegrass, revolutionized mandolin playing.
- Joe Val: 1960s New England-based, with Charles River Valley Boys, Lily Brothers, New England Bluegrass Boys.
- John Duffy: With 1950s and 1960s groups Country Gentleman and Seldom Scene, both newgrass pioneer bands.
- Ira Louvin: With 1940s and 1950s group the Louvin Brothers.

Jazz

- Jethro Burns: Part of the comedy team Homer and Jethro, pioneering jazz player.
- Tiny Moore: First famous electric jazz mandolin player with Bob Wills and His Texas Playboys.
- Dave Apollon: Russian born, perhaps the first jazz mandolin player, also played European folk and gypsy music, a legend in the mandolin world.

Classical

- Gabriele Leone: Mid 1700s virtuoso European mandolinist, wrote a method book and composed pieces demanding split-string technique (see Tip #33).
- Carlo Munier: Late 1800s, helped legitimize mandolin as a classical instrument.
- Raffaele Calace: Classical virtuoso in the second half of the 19th century, composed hundreds of pieces for mandolin, also famous as a builder of Neapolitan mandolins, made important structural improvements.
- Giuseppe Pettine: Classical performer and composer of many mandolin works in the early 1900s. Also famous for mandolin instructional books; worked with Vega to create excellent mandolins.
- Silvio Ranieri: A popular contemporary of Munier in Europe, also wrote a mandolin method book.
- Sam Siegel and Vittorio Monti: Classical mandolin heroes of late 19th to early 20th century.
- Bernardo de Pace: Called the "Wizard of the Mandolin," an American who played for the Metropolitan Opera and vaudeville in the 1920s and 1930s!

Blues

- Yank Rachell: Played with Sleepy John Estes, Sonny Boy Williamson, and Taj Mahal.
- Howard "Louie Bluie" Armstrong: Played with Estes and with the Tennessee Chocolate Drops.
- Carl Martin and Johnny Young: Played blues mandolin on Chicago's South Side in the 1950s.

91 KNOW YOUR MANDOLIN MASTERS PRESENT

Bluegrass

- Jesse McReynolds: Bluegrass pioneer with Jim and Jesse, a "golden age" band, innovator with his McReynolds crosspicking and split-string styles.
- Ronnie McCoury: Of the Del McCoury Band.
- Tim O'Brien: Played with Hot Rize, his sister Mollie, and many others.
- Bobby Osborne of the Osborne Brothers: They were among the 1950s "Golden Age of Bluegrass" bands.
- Frank Wakefield: Early on, played with Red Allen, Jimmy Martin, and the Greenbriar Boys.
- Roland White: Played with Kentucky Colonels, Lester Flatt, Nashville Bluegrass Band, and many others
- Sam Bush: Newgrass pioneer with the Newgrass Revival, has played with countless cutting-edge bluegrass and country luminaries.
- Rhonda Vincent: Leads her own bluegrass band.
- Marty Stuart: A country star who began by playing mandolin with Lester Flatt at age 14.
- Doyle Lawson: With Jimmy Martin in the '60s, Country Gentlemen in the '70s, Quicksilver in the '80s.
- Ricky Skaggs: Country star/multi-instrumentalist, played mandolin with Ralph Stanley, the Country Gentlemen, J. D. Crowe and the New South, Emmylou Harris's Hot Band and his own country band.

Jazz

- David Grisman: After playing with two bluegrass supergroups, Old and in the Way and Muleskinner, invented "Dawg Music" in the late 1970s, a mixture of gypsy jazz and bluegrass; long association with Jerry Garcia as well.
- Sam Bush: (see Bluegrass)
- Chris Thile: (see Multi-Genre)

Irish

- Andy Irvine: With Planxty band, Patrick Street, and many more Irish stars.
- Bob Schmidt: With Flogging Molly, Los Angeles-based Irish punk band.

Classical

Peter Ostroushko: Rumanian virtuoso who has composed many orchestral pieces, also recorded with pop and country stars, plays on *Prairie Home Companion*.

- Caterina Lichtenberg: Bulgarian classical mandolinist.

Multi-Genre

- Chris Thile of Punch Brothers and Nickel Creek: Arguably the most cutting-edge player today; plays bluegrass, jazz, classical, pop.

- Mike Marshall: Plays bluegrass, jazz, classical, Brazilian, with the band Montreux, and with Darol Anger, and most contemporary acoustic music stars, from the 1980s on.

- Andy Statman: From the 1980s on, bluegrass multi-instrumentalist played in pioneering newgrass bands Country Cooking and Breakfast Special, became a klezmer expert, has played with Itzhak Perlman and Béla Fleck.

- Marilynn Mair: American classical virtuoso, also plays choro.

- Caterina Lichtengerg: (see Classical) Also plays choro.

- U. Shrinivas: Plays Indian music and American jazz on electric mandolin.

- Radim Zenki: Czech mandolinist who plays bluegrass, jazz, and ethnic music; uses a fingerpick and a thumbpick to play tremolo melody and accompaniment at the same time!

- John Reischman: Plays bluegrass, jazz, and choro.

Blues

- Rich DelGrosso: Writer/teacher/performer, today's leading exponent of blues mandolin.

- Ry Cooder: Multi-string American roots music and world music maven, and film scorer; has played blues mandolin on various projects.

- Steve James: Multi-instrumentalist/teacher/performer; emphasizes blues on mandolin as well as guitar and banjo.

- Andra Faye: Mandolin/fiddler/teacher/performer; played with all-female blues band Saffire, as well as Andra Faye and the Mighty Good Men.

The European *gittern*, a late 13th century cousin of the lute*, may be an early ancestor of the mandolin. The body was teardrop shaped and it had four (sometimes three or five) string courses tuned to high pitches. The 16th century *mandore* (a similar instrument shaped like a mandolin, but with four single strings) was popular in France and came to Italy around 1660, where it was called a *mandola*, possibly because of the body's almond shape (*mandorla* is the Italian word for almond). Various Italian versions had four string courses in a high register. During the baroque era, 1600 to1750, the instrument was in wide use and was being called a *mandola* or *mandolino*. It was incorporated into Scarlatti's works, Vivaldi's concertos, and in opera arias and oratorios.

Also around this time, a four-coursed mandolin with metal strings—made in Naples—became very popular. A great deal of music was written for it and performed all over Europe by Italian and French performers and composers. This was to become the Neapolitan, roundback mandolin that we know today. Because it had metal strings, it was plucked with a stiff, tortoise shell pick rather than a feather. This arrangement leant itself to the tremolo technique (Tip #47) that is such a trademark sound of the mandolin. By 1800 the instrument's popularity subsided except for its use in popular music in Italy.

Around the end of the 19th century, virtuoso players like Carlo Munieri, Silvio Ranieri, and Vittorio Monti popularized the mandolin again. They performed all over Europe, published their compositions, and wrote instruction manuals. This became known as the "Golden Age of Mandolin"—during the late Romantic period—when the instrument was widely used in classical music.

By the 1920s, roundback mandolins had come to the U.S. and Gibson began manufacturing flatbacks. These were louder, sturdier, and well suited to rural string band music as well as classical music. Mandolin orchestras proliferated and the mandolin also became a staple in country music.

Today, the mandolin is most commonly heard in country and bluegrass and occasionally in pop or blues music. However, there has also been a resurgence of mandolin orchestras and the instrument is showing up in international genres like Irish and Brazilian choro music (see Tips #93 – 100).

The dates in the first few paragraphs of Tip #92 are approximate as many sources contradict each other by as much as a century.

Since the modern mandolin evolved from various related instruments in Italy, there is a centuries-old oral tradition of Italian folk music in which the mandolin plays an important role. Mandolin-driven songs, serenades, tarantellas, and other pieces were extremely popular throughout Italy in the late 1800s, a time when many Italians immigrated to the U.S. The bowl-backed (Neapolitan) mandolins and the Italian songs associated with them became very popular and the mandolin was one of the first instruments to be recorded on Edison cylinders, the predecessor of "records."

Unlike classical mandolin music that flourished during the late 19th century, very little popular or traditional mandolin music was written down. Alan Lomax, the great folk musicologist, traveled throughout Italy in the 1950s and recorded street singers and rural performers. Over the years, more and more of these traditional sounds have been notated and recorded.

Pop tunes like "Volaré" and "Love Theme from 'The Godfather'" were written in a style that emulates and evokes the sound of these old songs. Traditional Italian mandolin music includes mazurkas, waltzes, marches, tangos, polkas, tarantellas, and more. As one might expect, various regions of Italy are noted for different musical genres. As is true all over the world, some of the folk tunes fulfilled specific ritual needs. The serenade was to be played after sundown as "sera" means evening, and it was considered a courtship song. Tarantellas go back as far as the 1600s and were originally written for a medicinal/religious exorcism dance, designed to cure the victim of a tarantula bite!

94 MANDOLIN IN BLUEGRASS AND OLD-TIME MUSIC

Old-time music is another name for Southern string band music. Record companies coined the expression "old-time" in the early 1920s to label rural, white, unschooled, and unpolished music that was (and still is) performed mostly on stringed instruments. The usual instruments were guitar, fiddle, banjo, mandolin, and bass or gutbucket or jug. Harmonicas and other non-stringed instruments sometimes chimed in.

Mandolin players in old-time string bands play solos and rhythmic, strummed accompaniment, often employing the tremolo technique derived from Italian mandolin styles.

Bluegrass didn't gel as a musical genre until the late 1940s when mandolin player/tenor singer Bill Monroe organized a string band that was markedly different from old-time bands. For example, during a song, soloists took turns playing instrumentals, which encouraged virtuosic playing. Also, the harmony singing was very organized, often along the lines of Baptist church vocalizing. Monroe also featured Earl Scruggs with his fast, rolling, banjo style and he dressed the band in dignified matching suits. He also refrained from performing hillbilly humor, a mainstay of many old-time acts.

Many bands sprang up imitating Monroe's format, and the public began referring to them as "bluegrass" bands because they sounded like Bill Monroe and His Bluegrass Boys (so named because Bill was from the bluegrass region of Kentucky). By the 1950s, now known as the golden age of bluegrass, Monroe-style music was an established genre, an offshoot of country music that harked back to the older, rural styles, as it was performed acoustically — no electric instruments and no drums, and all strings.

The typical bluegrass band consists of a guitar, a bass, a banjo, a fiddle, and a mandolin. A Dobro is considered optional. Some bluegrass bands have a fiddle or a mandolin, but not both, as the two instruments share the same tuning and have a similar musical function in a band. They both play solos and background licks (behind singers) and often provide rhythmic "chops" — staccato chords that punctuate the backbeats in 4/4 time. Also, the mandolin can sustain a note by playing a long tremolo, just as the fiddle sustains a note with the bow.

95 MANDOLIN IN COUNTRY MUSIC AND BROTHER ACTS

"Brother Acts" proliferated in country music in the 1930s and 40s, and often one of the brothers played mandolin. Their music was more polished than much of the string band music of their time and the close sibling harmony added a special appeal. Some of the more popular groups were the Delmore Brothers, Louvin Brothers, Monroe Brothers, the Blue Sky Boys, the Maddox Brothers and Rose, the Morris Brothers, the Rouse Brothers, the Dixon Brothers, and Sam and Kirk McGee.

Of the above-mentioned acts, the Louvin Brothers, Monroe Brothers, and Blue Sky Boys are of particular interest to mandolin players, as the mandolin was prominent in many of their hits and they were a big influence on countless country and bluegrass stars. The Monroe Brothers included Bill Monroe, now universally acknowledged as the father of bluegrass music.

Many early bluegrass bands were led by brothers including: the Stanley Brothers, The Osborne Brothers, Jim and Jesse McReynolds, and the Goins Brothers.

Just like in bluegrass, the mandolin has been featured often in country music as a background texture or a soloing instrument and is still heard in contemporary pop-country recordings. Recent bands and artists featuring the mandolin include the Dixie Chicks, Sugarland, Brooks and Dunn, Little Big Town, the Cowboy Junkies, Randy Travis, Taylor Swift, and Zac Brown.

96 MANDOLIN IN CLASSICAL MUSIC

The mandolin has a rich history in classical music. Beethoven played mandolin! However, that's just a start. In the Baroque era (1600-1750), mandolin was featured in chamber works along with lutes, harpsichord, harp, and bowed stringed instruments. It was often the highest-pitched instrument and was used to play the single-note melodic lines. Many European composers wrote for mandolin during this time.

In the 18th century, the European aristocracy favored the mandolin and original works were written for it by Mozart, Beethoven, Bizet, Vivaldi (who wrote both a single and a double mandolin concerto) and many other famous composers.

The late 19th century to early 20th century is called the "Golden Age of Mandolin" because of virtuoso players/composers like Carlo Munier, from Florence, whose "Capriccioso Spagnolo" is still one of the most-performed classical mandolin pieces. Silvio Ranieri was popular all over Europe and, like Munier, wrote a mandolin method book. Raffaele Calace, Giuseppe Pettine, Sam Siegel, and Vittorio Monti are also mandolin heroes of this period.

From 1890 to 1920, mandolin orchestras performed in every major metropolis in America. By the 1920s this craze subsided, but some mandolin orchestras continued to exist and the 1980s saw a strong revival. Dozens of such ensembles now perform all over the U.S., playing classical, ragtime, folk, and even pop music. Many of them include the mandola, mandocello, and mandobass.

97 MANDOLIN IN CHORO MUSIC

Brazilian choro music is a virtuosic, instrumental, acoustic style, which combines African rhythms and European dance music, sometimes echoing the harmonic and melodic aspects of ragtime. It is often played in a rapid, upbeat tempo in 2/4 time. This rather eclectic genre, which predates samba and bossa nova, evolved in late 19th century and many say it expresses the soul of Brazil more than any other music.

A typical choro ensemble includes a flute or clarinet, a guitar, a seven-string guitar that plays bass lines, a percussion instrument called a pandeiro that resembles a tambourine, and other stringed instruments, including the bandolim, which is the Brazilian flatback mandolin. The bandolim often plays the melodies making it a very important part of the choro sound.

Like bluegrass, choro has never achieved the success bestowed upon pop music, but it has the respect of many world-famous musicians and a fervent fan base that keep reviving its popularity from time to time. Many highly acclaimed mandolin players have recently been performing, recording, and spreading the gospel of choro all over the world, including American bluegrass/world music virtuoso Mike Marshall, the Bulgarian classical mandolinist, Caterina Lichtenberg, and American classical virtuoso Marilyn Mair.

98 MANDOLIN IN POP MUSIC

Occasionally, mandolin provides the "hook" in pop and rock songs (the repeated lick that sticks in your head) or it strums along in the background, or provides long tremolo lines beneath a vocalist. Several pop songs over the years have featured the mandolin including:

- "Boat on the River" (Styx)
- "Friend of the Devil" and "Ripple" (Grateful Dead with David Grisman)
- "Going to California" and "Battle of Evermore" (Led Zeppelin)
- "Lady Rain" (Hall and Oates)
- "Losing My Religion" (REM)
- "Mandolin Wind" and "Maggie May" (Rod Stewart)
- "Mr. Bojangles" (Nitty Gritty Dirt Band)
- "Rag Mama Rag" (the Band)

Mandolin is often present in the music of these popular bands:

- Barenaked Ladies — Kevin Hearn
- Counting Crows — David Immerglück
- Cowboy Junkies — Jeff Bird
- Dropkick Murphys — Jeff DaRosa
- Flogging Molly — Robert Schmidt (aka Bob Schmidt)
- The Hooters — Eric Bazilian
- Mumford & Sons — Marcus Mumford
- Planxty — Andy Irvine
- The String Cheese Incident — Michael Kang
- Sugarland — Kristian Bush

99 IRISH MANDOLIN

The mandolin is a natural for playing Irish fiddle tunes (hornpipes, jigs and reels) because it is tuned exactly like a fiddle. Most Irish mandolin players favor the flatback, round-holed instrument. They play with a pick and—like the banjo player in Irish bands—play mostly single-string melodies. Not as loud as a banjo, Irish mandolin has only recently begun to gain popularity.

Andy Irvine (Planxty, Patrick Street), Dave Richardson (Boys of the Lough), Marla Fibish (Three Mile Stone), and Brian McGillicuddy (the Fuchsia Band) are well-known Irish mandolinists.

100 BLUES MANDOLIN

The mandolin has a rich blues tradition. As early as 1903, W. C. Handy, the great blues songwriter/publisher described a blues band he saw that consisted of a guitarist, a mandolinist, and a bassist. The earliest recordings of African-American string bands and jug bands often included the mandolin. On his blues mandolin-centric website, Rich DelGrosso makes the point that mandolin players helped shape both ragtime and the blues during the onset of recorded music.

Later blues recordings also feature acoustic or an electric mandolin. Muddy Waters' first Stovall Plantation recording, "Burr Clover Blues," in the 1940s, included Louis Ford on mandolin. Yank Rachell recorded and performed with Sleepy John Estes and Sonny Boy Williamson in the 1930s. Howard "Louie Bluie" Armstrong played mandolin with Estes and as a member of the Tennessee Chocolate Drops. Carl Martin and Johnny Young played blues mandolin on Chicago's South Side in the 1950s. More recently, Ry Cooder, Rich DelGrosso, Steve James, Andra Faye, Billy Flynn, and other contemporary players steeped in traditional blues are keeping blues mandolin alive!

There are two documentary films about Howard Armstrong: *Louie Bluie* and *Sweet Old Song*. Yank Rachell also appears in *Louie Bluie*. Armstrong kept performing and recording, often with younger musicians, into the 1990s.

101 MANDOLIN MAKERS

For bluegrass and classical mandolinists, the most sought-after instruments are the Gibson F-5s (like Bill Monroe's mandolin) made during the 1920s under the supervision of Lloyd Loar. However, if you're not keen on spending $200,000, there are other options.

Many foreign-made, entry-level mandolins sell for under $500. Some try to look like expensive instruments, but are poorly made and hard to play. Others are stripped-down, less fancy looking instruments that have good action and are easy to play. Eastman and Kentucky have some good starter mandolins.

Kentucky, Aria, Washburn, and Ibanez make slightly better mandolins in the $500 – $700 range with solid wood (rather than laminated) backs, tops, and sides. Getting closer to the $1000 range, Flatiron makes good A models. Collings, Breedlove, and Michael Kelly make higher-end models, as does Gibson.

Browse **www.mandolincafe.com** and similar mandolin sites to find people comparing notes about their instruments.